16-19
MATHEMATICS

D1144290

The Normal distribution

The School Mathematics Project

The right of the
University of Cambridge
to print and sell
all manner of books
was granted by
Henry VIII in 1534.
The University has printed
and published continuously
since 1584.

Cambridge University Press

Cambridge   New York   Port Chester   Melbourne   Sydney

Main authors	Chris Belsom
	Robert Black
	David Cundy
	Stan Dolan
	Chris Little
	Fiona McGill
	Mary Rouncefield
	Jane Southern
Team leader	Chris Belsom
Project director	Stan Dolan
Statistics programs	Margaret and Peter Hayball

The authors would like to give special thanks to Ann White for her help in producing the trial edition and in preparing this book for publication.

Published by the Press Syndicate of the University of Cambridge
The Pitt Building, Trumpington Street, Cambridge CB2 1RP
40 West 20th Street, New York, NY10011–4211, USA
10 Stamford Road, Oakleigh, Victoria 3166, Australia

© Cambridge University Press 1992

First published 1992

Printed in Great Britain at the University Press, Cambridge

Produced by Gecko Limited, Bicester, Oxon

Cartoons by Tony Hall

Cover photography by Tick Ahearn

Cover design by Iguana Creative Design

British Library cataloguing in publication data
A catalogue record for this book may be obtained from the British Library

ISBN 0 521 40890 3

Contents

1 An important distribution

1.1 Introduction

Variability is an important feature of life – without it there would be little call for a study of probability and statistics! In this unit you will consider whether there are patterns in this variability and whether or not you can describe the patterns mathematically.

Stand on any busy street corner and you cannot fail to notice the immense variety in the human form.

Suppose you were asked to sample the heights of 100 adult males and draw a histogram. Jot down the rough shape of the histogram you would expect.

Why would you expect to get the shape you have drawn?

Tasksheet 1 considers the variety in the weights of different 2p coins.

TASKSHEET 1 — Coins (page 15)

Many frequency distributions look like those for the weights of coins.

- The frequency distribution is approximately symmetrical.

- Most of the values are grouped around the mean.

- Values a long way from the mean are not very likely.

1.2 A pattern emerges!

It is interesting to consider whether the distributions of other variable quantities have the same or similar shapes.

TASKSHEET 2 — Different variables (page 16)

> Comment on the shapes of the various distributions considered in the tasksheet, describing their similarities and differences.
>
> Which distributions have the same shape as that for the weights of coins?

Although the data sets are of different sorts of observation the distributions have approximately the same shape (data set E is the exception). Most of the values are near the mean, which is in the middle, and the distribution is roughly symmetrical. It is often described as being 'bell-shaped'.

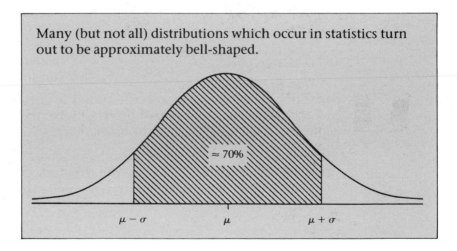

Many (but not all) distributions which occur in statistics turn out to be approximately bell-shaped.

$\approx 70\%$

$\mu - \sigma \qquad \mu \qquad \mu + \sigma$

As well as the distributions having similar shapes, the proportion of the data contained within 1 standard deviation of the mean is approximately the same (about 70%) for each data set.

Your work so far might lead you to suspect that there is, or might be, a common underlying distribution for various physical situations. If there is, then perhaps it is possible to find a suitable mathematical model to describe it. This approach is pursued first by considering a method of **standardising the data** and then by making the **area** under each histogram independent of the total frequency.

5

1.3 Standardising the data

A group of students sat examinations in both mathematics and economics.

> Debbie scored 64 for mathematics and 78 for economics.
>
> Which was the better result?

The class results were as follows:

- The mathematics scores had mean 54 and standard deviation 4.8.
- The economics scores had mean 68 and standard deviation 8.0.

In comparing two examination scores, working out how far each is above or below the mean takes account of the difference in means, but not the difference in spread. To take account of this, you can measure the distance from the mean in **units of standard deviation**. So, for Debbie,

- her mathematics score was $\dfrac{(64 - 54)}{4.8} = 2.08$ standard deviations above the mean;

- her economics score was $\dfrac{(78 - 68)}{8.0} = 1.25$ standard deviations above the mean;

These results, 2.08 and 1.25, are called the **standardised** scores, and give a simple method of comparison. The higher the standardised score, the better the examination performance.

Standardised data is often denoted by the variable Z. (It is sometimes referred to as the z-score.) It is conventional to use capital letters for random variables and lower case letters for their values.

> Suppose a data set has mean $\bar{x}$ and standard deviation s. The standardised value of an observation x is z, where
> $$z = \frac{x - \bar{x}}{s}$$

Suppose eight competitors in a school quiz programme have scores of 9, 9, 10, 12, 14, 16, 16 and 18.

The mean score is $\dfrac{104}{8}$ = 13. The standard deviation is 3.28 (to 3 s.f.).

The **standardised** form of the score of 9 is $\dfrac{9 - 13}{3.28}$ = −1.22 (to 3 s.f.).

This means that the score of 9 is 1.22 standard deviation units **below** the mean.

The full set of standardised scores is as follows:

Original score	9	9	10	12	14	16	16	18
Standardised score		−1.22	−1.22	−0.915	−0.305	0.305	0.915	0.915	1.52

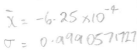

$\bar{x} = -6.25 \times 10^{-4}$

$\sigma = 0.990571727$

The mean of the standardised scores for the data set is 0.00, and the standard deviation is 1.00 (to 3 s.f.).

The calculations could be performed conveniently on a computer spreadsheet or with a statistics 'package' on the computer. You might like to try this or you could write a short program to do the job for you on a programmable calculator or computer.

> The mean and the standard deviation of the standardised scores are approximately 0 and 1 respectively for this data set.
>
> Investigate other small data sets and comment on your findings.

A standardised data set has a mean of 0 and a standard deviation of 1.

EXERCISE 1

1   Standardise

   (a) a score of 6 from a population of mean 8 and standard deviation 2;

   (b) a score of 1.45 from a population of mean 2.3 and standard deviation 0.3;

   (c) a score of 3.4 from a population of mean 0 and standard deviation 3.4;

   (d) a score of x from a population of mean m and standard deviation d.

2   (a) By calculating the standardised scores, compare the results of the following students in mathematics and economics. The results for the full entry of students in mathematics had a mean of 54 and a standard deviation of 4.8. For economics, there was a mean of 68 and a standard deviation of 8.

	Mathematics	Economics
Karen	58	71
Alex	41	41
Melanie	54	68
Chris	20	25

   (b) Cindy did equally well in economics and mathematics. If she scored 64 marks in mathematics, what were her economics marks?

   (c) Mark obtained the same mark in each subject, and his performances were equally good. What marks did he get?

3   A population of men has a mean height of 5 ft 8 in and standard deviation 2.8 inches. A population of women has a mean height of 5 ft 6 in and standard deviation 2.4 inches.

   (a) Which is taller (relative to his or her own population), a 5 ft 7 in man or a 5 ft 5 in woman?

   (b) . What woman's height, to the nearest inch, is equivalent to that of a 6 ft man?

1.4 Considering the area

Standardised data sets have the same mean and variance. To make comparisons between data sets even more meaningful you can also make the area under the graph of each distribution the same.

You should recall that, for a histogram,

$$\text{height of a block} = \text{frequency density} = \frac{\text{frequency}}{\text{width of interval}}$$

For example, consider the data below for the weights of one hundred 2p coins.

Weight (g)	6.8–7.0	7.0–7.1	7.1–7.2	7.2–7.3	7.3–7.5
Frequency	8	29	46	12	5

The histogram is:

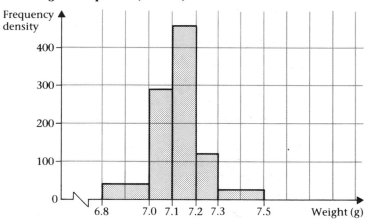

The weights of 2p coins (n = 100)

What does the **area** of each block represent?   *frequency of class*

What does the total area of all the blocks represent?   *total frequency*

To make area independent of total frequency, consider the **relative frequency** in each class, which is simply the frequency for each class divided by the total frequency.

$$\text{relative frequency} = \frac{\text{frequency for the class}}{\text{total frequency}}$$

The height of each block on the histogram now becomes:

$$\text{height} = \frac{\text{relative frequency}}{\text{width of interval}} = \text{relative frequency density}$$

The relative frequency density histogram for the coins can now be drawn using the data given below.

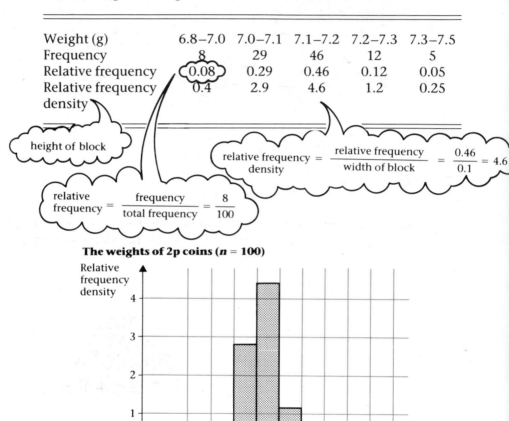

Weight (g)	6.8–7.0	7.0–7.1	7.1–7.2	7.2–7.3	7.3–7.5
Frequency	8	29	46	12	5
Relative frequency	0.08	0.29	0.46	0.12	0.05
Relative frequency density	0.4	2.9	4.6	1.2	0.25

height of block

relative frequency density $= \dfrac{\text{relative frequency}}{\text{width of block}} = \dfrac{0.46}{0.1} = 4.6$

relative frequency $= \dfrac{\text{frequency}}{\text{total frequency}} = \dfrac{8}{100}$

The weights of 2p coins (_n_ = 100)

Relative frequency density

What is the total relative frequency?

What is the total area of the histogram?

Draw the relative frequency density histogram for one of the data sets A–E from datasheet 1. Confirm that the total area is 1.

A relative frequency density histogram has a total area of 1.

1.5 The 'Normal' curve

You have seen that many, **but not all**, data sets have an approximately bell-shaped histogram. This has been observed and noted by many mathematicians, among them Carl Friedrich Gauss (1777–1855) and Abraham de Moivre (1667–1754).

Gauss noted that 'errors' in scientific measurement produced the bell-shaped histogram. He hypothesised that measurements which are subject to accidental or random effects will always produce a histogram of this shape.

The histogram below illustrates a very large data set where the data are grouped into small block widths. The data represent the mass (kg) of new-born babies.

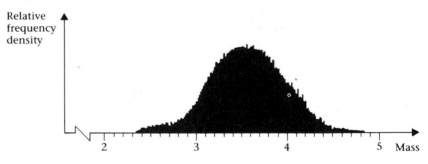

The histogram has a fairly smooth bell shape and it is natural to draw a smooth curve through the tops of the blocks.

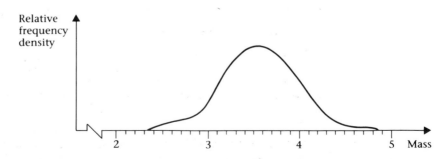

You can model this curve approximately with the graph of a symmetrical function.

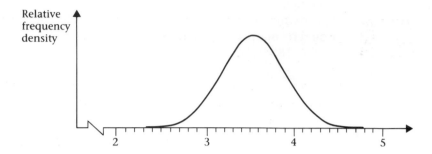

The sketch shows the bell-shaped distribution which has provided the skeleton shape for many distributions. A mathematical model for such distributions was developed by de Moivre and Laplace (1749–1827). It was upon this model that Gauss, de Moivre and Laplace based their theory of errors. For this reason, the bell-shaped curve is sometimes called the 'Gaussian error curve'. It is more commonly known as the **Normal curve.**

When a data set has been standardised, the particular Normal curve which models the data takes on a number of important properties. The Normal curve for standardised data is called the **Standard Normal curve**.

> Describe the shape and area properties of the Standard Normal curve. *Bell shaped, Symm abt mean, area = 1.*

To make full use of this mathematical model to describe data sets you need to identify the function involved. This is investigated in the next section.

The Standard Normal distribution has mean 0 and standard deviation 1.

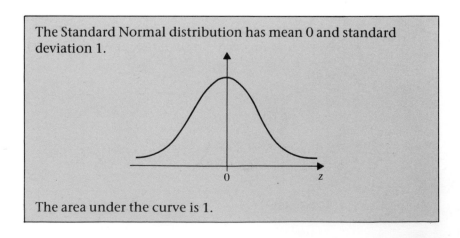

The area under the curve is 1.

1.6 Finding the function

Plot the graphs of functions of the form

$$f(x) = ke^{-\frac{1}{2}x^2}$$

and show that functions of this form have the same basic **shape** as the Normal curve. Consider different values of k, including negative values.

What other important **area** property should the function possess? How does this help in finding the required value of k?

The function f, where

$$f(x) = ke^{-\frac{1}{2}x^2}$$

has the basic shape of the Normal curve. (k is a positive constant, as yet undetermined.)

Sketches of the graph of f for various values of k are shown below.

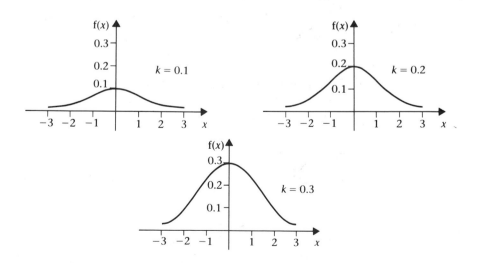

Each curve has the correct shape. It is necessary only to find which curve encloses an area of 1.

TASKSHEET 3 — Area under the Normal curve (page 17)

13

The numerical methods employed on tasksheet 3 give a value for k of approximately 0.4. In fact, it can be shown that the precise value for k is $\dfrac{1}{\sqrt{2\pi}}$.

The equation of the Standard Normal curve is

$$f(x) = \frac{1}{\sqrt{2\pi}}\, e^{-\frac{1}{2}x^2}$$

After working through this chapter you should:

1   know how to standardise a data set;

2   know that standardised data have mean 0 and standard deviation 1;

3   know that a relative frequency density histogram has a total area of 1;

4   appreciate that the Normal distribution is often a good model for real data sets. You should remember, however, that even if the distribution **is** bell-shaped the Normal curve may be only an **approximate** fit. The fit should be good enough to obtain useful information from the use of a Normal model.

5   know that the mathematical description for the Standard Normal function, $f(x)$ is

$$f(x) = \frac{1}{\sqrt{2\pi}}\, e^{-\frac{1}{2}x^2}$$

6   know that the area under the Standard Normal curve is 1;

7   know that the Standard Normal distribution has mean 0 and standard deviation 1.

Coins

You will need the weights of 100 2p coins and recording sheet 1: *Coins*. Weights should be obtained either by weighing 100 coins on an electronic balance or by using the data provided below.

Weights of 100 2p coins (grams)

7.15	7.08	7.09	7.05	7.33
7.05	7.09	7.12	7.18	7.19
7.08	7.09	7.09	7.20	7.07
7.12	7.11	7.26	6.86	7.14
6.80	7.11	6.99	7.05	7.11
7.27	6.97	7.40	7.12	7.44
7.17	7.17	7.05	7.18	7.13
7.11	7.19	7.16	7.04	7.15
7.11	7.01	7.21	7.02	7.05
7.03	7.22	7.30	7.18	7.14
7.08	7.06	7.30	7.12	7.04
7.11	7.16	7.07	7.22	7.18
7.24	7.20	7.09	7.13	7.11
6.95	7.01	7.18	7.23	7.16
7.00	7.08	7.03	7.04	7.18
7.17	7.12	7.14	7.13	7.18
7.19	7.07	6.98	7.22	7.15
7.34	7.18	7.21	7.06	7.24
6.98	7.25	7.19	7.29	7.17
7.20	7.04	7.17	7.19	7.11

1 Group the data into the frequency distribution shown on the recording sheet and complete the table.

2 Draw a frequency distribution diagram for the data and comment on its shape.

3 Using the frequency distribution, show that the mean and standard deviation of the weights in grams of the 2p coins are 7.1 and 0.10 (correct to 2 s.f.).

4 What proportion of the observations (**approximately**) are

(a) within ± 1 standard deviation of the mean;

(b) more than 2 standard deviations from the mean.

Different variables

Choose **one** of the data sets on datasheet 1: *Different variables*, making sure that each of the data sets A–E is considered by someone in the class. Alternatively, you may choose to collect a similar data set of your own.

1 Draw a frequency distribution to represent the data. You should collect the data into groups whose widths are all 1 standard deviation. For example, if the data have mean 10.3 and standard deviation 0.2, use intervals of:

... 9.9 – 10.1   10.1 – 10.3   10.3 – 10.5 ...

2 What proportion of the observations for your chosen data set

(a) are within 1 standard deviation of the mean;

(b) are between 1 and 2 standard deviations above the mean;

(c) are more than 3 standard deviations away from the mean?

3 Obtain from others in your class results for all the data sets and copy and complete the table below.

Data set	Approximate proportion of observations within n standard deviations of the mean			
	±1	±2	±3	beyond 3
A				
B				
C				
D				
E				

Area under the Normal curve

1   For the graph of $g = e^{-\frac{1}{2}x^2}$

  (a) use the program *Traprule*, or write a short program for your calculator, to estimate the total area under the curve,

  (b) estimate the proportion of the area under the curve between

    (i) 0 and 1   (ii) 1 and 2   (iii) 2 and 3;

  (c) write down the corresponding proportions between 0 and -1, between -1 and -2 and between -2 and -3.

2   Compare your results for data sets A–D on tasksheet 2 with your answers to question 1.

In order to model the relative frequency density histograms for the data sets, the total area under the curve must equal 1. This can be done by considering a function of the form

$$ke^{-\frac{1}{2}x^2}$$

where k is an appropriate constant.

3   The total area under $e^{-\frac{1}{2}x^2}$ was estimated in question 1(a). Investigate other functions $ke^{-\frac{1}{2}x^2}$ for various k until you find the value of k which makes the total area equal to 1.

2 The Normal distribution

2.1 Introduction

You have seen how the Normal curve can be used as a model for the distribution of a number of continuous variables. How can you use this information?

EXAMPLE 1

Over a long period of time a farmer notes that the eggs produced by his chickens have a mean weight of 60 g, and a standard deviation of 15 g. If eggs are classified by weight and small eggs are those having a weight of less than 45 g then what proportion of his eggs will be classsified as small?

SOLUTION

Assume that the distribution of the weight of the eggs is Normal, having mean 60 g and standard deviation 15 g.

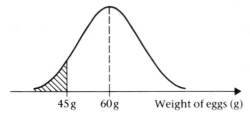

45 g is 1 standard deviation below the mean. You know that 70% (approximately) of the weights will be within ± 1 standard deviation of the mean.

From the diagram you can see that about 15% of his eggs will be small.

> Use your knowledge of areas under the Normal curve to find the proportion of eggs having weights between 60 g and 75 g.

2.2 Area and probability

You saw in *Living with uncertainty* that relative frequency provides an estimate of probability.

The standardised Normal function, which you have used to model data sets, is also known as the **Normal probability density function**.

With relative frequency density histograms, the area of a block represents the relative frequency of occurrence of the values in the particular interval.

For the Normal distribution, the area shaded is the probability of obtaining a value of x between a and b.

$$\text{Area} = P(a \leq x \leq b)$$

It is possible to obtain any such area by numerical integration in a similar way to that which you used when investigating the mathematical form of the Normal function.

EXERCISE 1

Use numerical integration techniques to complete this exercise.

1 Copy and complete the table below, which gives the approximate area under

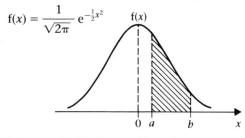

$$f(x) = \frac{1}{\sqrt{2\pi}} \, e^{-\frac{1}{2}x^2}$$

a	b	Area
0	1	0.341
1	2	0.136
2	3	0.0215

between the limits a and b as shown.

2 Use the symmetry property of the curve to write down the areas enclosed between ±1, ±2, ±3 standard deviations of the mean.

3 For the Standard Normal curve write down estimates of the probability of obtaining a value of x which is

(a) between ± 1 standard deviation of the mean;

(b) more than 2 standard deviations away from the mean;

(c) more than 3 standard deviations above the mean.

2.3 Tables for the Normal function

Using numerical methods, accurate tables have been constructed for the area under the Normal curve. A typical table is shown below.

z	.00	.01	.02	.03	.04	.05	.06	.07	.08	.09
0.0	.5000	.5040	.5080	.5120	.5160	.5199	.5239	.5279	.5319	.5359
0.1	.5398	.5438	.5478	.5517	.5557	.5596	.5636	.5675	.5714	.5753
0.2	.5793	.5832	.5871	.5910	.5948	.5987	.6026	.6064	.6103	.6141
0.3	.6179	.6217	.6255	.6293	.6331	.6368	.6406	.6443	.6480	.6517
0.4	.6554	.6591	.6628	.6664	.6700	.6736	.6772	.6808	.6844	.6879
0.5	.6915	.6950	.6985	.7019	.7054	.7088	.7123	.7157	.7190	.7224
0.6	.7257	.7291	.7324	.7357	.7389	.7422	.7454	.7486	.7517	.7549
0.7	.7580	.7611	.7642	.7673	.7704	.7734	.7764	.7794	.7823	.7852
0.8	.7881	.7910	.7939	.7967	.7995	.8023	.8051	.8078	.8106	.8133
0.9	.8159	.8186	.8212	.8238	.8264	.8289	.8315	.8340	.8365	.8389
1.0	.8413	.8438	.8461	.8485	.8508	.8531	.8554	.8577	.8599	.8621
1.1	.8643	.8665	.8686	.8708	.8729	.8749	.8770	.8790	.8810	.8830
1.2	.8849	.8869	.8888	.8907	.8925	.8944	.8962	.8980	.8997	.9015
1.3	.9032	.9049	.9066	.9082	.9099	.9115	.9131	.9147	.9162	.9177
1.4	.9192	.9207	.9222	.9236	.9251	.9265	.9279	.9292	.9306	.9319
1.5	.9332	.9345	.9357	.9370	.9382	.9394	.9406	.9418	.9429	.9441
1.6	.9452	.9463	.9474	.9484	.9495	.9505	.9515	.9525	.9535	.9545
1.7	.9554	.9564	.9573	.9582	.9591	.9599	.9608	.9616	.9625	.9633
1.8	.9641	.9649	.9656	.9664	.9671	.9678	.9686	.9693	.9699	.9706
1.9	.9713	.9719	.9726	.9732	.9738	.9744	.9750	.9756	.9761	.9767
2.0	.9772	.9778	.9783	.9788	.9793	.9798	.9803	.9808	.9812	.9817
2.1	.9821	.9826	.9830	.9834	.9838	.9842	.9846	.9850	.9854	.9857
2.2	.9861	.9864	.9868	.9871	.9875	.9878	.9881	.9884	.9887	.9890
2.3	.9893	.9896	.9898	.9901	.9904	.9906	.9909	.9911	.9913	.9916
2.4	.9918	.9920	.9922	.9925	.9927	.9929	.9931	.9932	.9934	.9936
2.5	.9938	.9940	.9941	.9943	.9945	.9946	.9948	.9949	.9951	.9952
2.6	.9953	.9955	.9956	.9957	.9959	.9960	.9961	.9962	.9963	.9964
2.7	.9965	.9966	.9967	.9968	.9969	.9970	.9971	.9972	.9973	.9974
2.8	.9974	.9975	.9976	.9977	.9977	.9978	.9979	.9979	.9980	.9981
2.9	.9981	.9982	.9982	.9983	.9984	.9984	.9985	.9985	.9986	.9986
3.0	.9987	.9987	.9987	.9988	.9988	.9989	.9989	.9989	.9990	.9990
3.1	.9990	.9991	.9991	.9991	.9992	.9992	.9992	.9992	.9993	.9993
3.2	.9993	.9993	.9994	.9994	.9994	.9994	.9994	.9995	.9995	.9995
3.3	.9995	.9995	.9995	.9996	.9996	.9996	.9996	.9996	.9996	.9997
3.4	.9997	.9997	.9997	.9997	.9997	.9997	.9997	.9997	.9997	.9998

Joint Matriculation Board

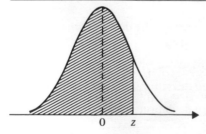

The table gives the area to the left of (or below) any given z value. This is best illustrated with a diagram. z is the number of standard deviation units from the mean value.

From the table you can see that the area to the left of $z = 2$ is 0.977 (to 3 s.f.).

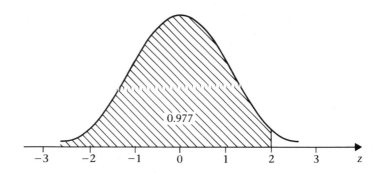

Using this information alone, what other areas can you find?

It is convenient to have a shorthand notation for the area under the curve up to a given standardised value z.

The area under the Standard Normal curve that is to the left of z is denoted by $\Phi(z)$.

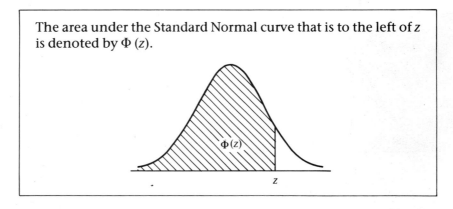

When solving problems using the Normal curve you should **always** start with a sketch to help you see exactly what is required.

E X A M P L E   2

Find the area under the Standard Normal curve

(a) between 1 and 2 standard deviations above the mean;

(b) more than 2 standard deviations above the mean;

(c) more than 1 standard deviation below the mean;

(d) between $-\frac{1}{2}$ and $+1$ standard deviation from the mean.

21

SOLUTION

(a)

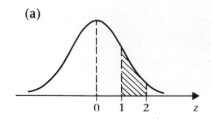

The area to the left of $z = 1$ is 0.8413
The area to the left of $z = 2$ is 0.9772
The shaded area $= 0.9772 - 0.8413$
$= 0.136$ (to 3 s.f.)

(b)

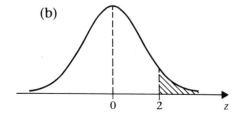

The area up to $z = 2$ is $\Phi(2) = 0.9772$
The area beyond $z = 2$ is $1 - 0.9772 = 0.0228$

since the total area under the curve has to be 1

(c)

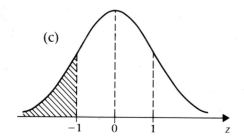

Using the symmetry property of the curve:

$\Phi(-1) = 1 - \Phi(+1)$
$= 1 - 0.841$
$= 0.159$

(d)

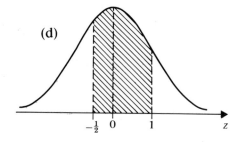

The required area is

(area up to $z = 1$) $-$ (area up to $z = -\frac{1}{2}$)
$= \Phi(+1) - \Phi(-\frac{1}{2})$

Now $\Phi(-0.5) = 1 - \Phi(0.5)$ (by symmetry)
$= 1 - 0.6915$
$= 0.3085$
and $\Phi(1) = 0.8413$
The shaded area $= 0.8413 - 0.3085$
$= 0.533$

E X E R C I S E   2

In each of the examples below, you should draw a sketch which shows the relevant area.

1   Using the table of areas under the Standard Normal curve, find

(a) the area between $z = 1$ and $z = 1.5$

(b) the area above

(i) $z = 1.5$

(ii) $z = -2$

(c) the area below

(i) $z = 1.62$

(ii) $z = 1.47$

(iii) $z = -1.6$

(d) the area enclosed between

(i) $z = 1.42$ and $z = 1.84$

(ii) $z = -1$ and $z = 1.5$

(iii) $z = -0.5$ and $z = -1.5$

2   Find the area enclosed between

(a) ± 1 standard deviation of the mean (between $z = 1$ and $z = -1$)

(b) ± 2 standard deviations of the mean

(c) ± 3 standard deviations of the mean

3   Find the value of z for which the area to the left of z is

(a) 0.8888   (b) 0.670   (c) 0.9332

(d) 0.484   (e) 0.1251

4   Find the value of z for which the area to the right of z is

(a) 0.9357   (b) 0.881   (c) 0.2206

(d) 0.3632   (e) 0.5279

2.4 **Normal distributions**

In chapter 1 of this unit you saw that any Normal curve can be reduced to the Standard Normal curve by standardising the variable. It is therefore possible to use the Standard Normal curve to solve problems for any Normally distributed variable.

Figures from the Office of Population Census and Surveys show that the mean height of British women (over 16 years) is 160.9 cm and the standard deviation is 6 cm. How would you find the proportion of British women over 166 cm tall?

Always start by illustrating the problem with a sketch.

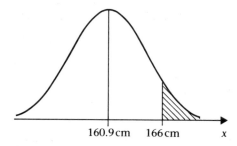

Note that 166 is about 1 s.d. above the mean.

Assuming that the heights are Normally distributed, approximately 68% of the population are within ± 1 s.d. of the mean.

Approximately what proportion of women will have a height greater than 166 cm?

17%.

You can tackle the problem more precisely in the following way.

First consider the distribution of female heights. The mean height is given as 160.9 cm and the standard deviation is 6 cm. You can assume that the distribution of heights is approximately Normal.

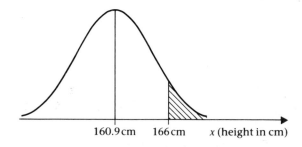

To find the proportion of women taller than 166 cm you need to find the area to the right of that value. In order to use the standard Normal tables, first convert the variable X to a **standardised normal variable** Z.

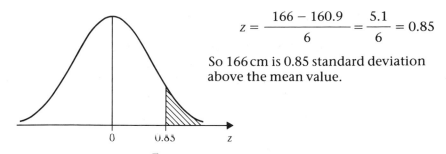

$$z = \frac{166 - 160.9}{6} = \frac{5.1}{6} = 0.85$$

So 166 cm is 0.85 standard deviation above the mean value.

The area of the left of $Z = 0.85$ is 0.8023 (from tables).

So over 80.2% of women are shorter than 166 cm. Conversely it follows that just less than 20% of women will be taller than 166 cm. This should compare reasonably well with your earlier estimate.

If a variable X has a distribution which is modelled by a Normal function, and X has mean μ and standard deviation σ, then

$$X \sim N(\mu, \sigma^2)$$

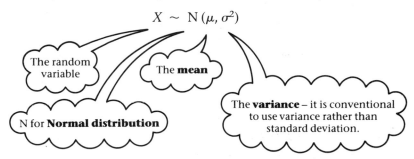

The **random variable**

The **mean**

N for **Normal distribution**

The **variance** – it is conventional to use variance rather than standard deviation.

This is a standard notation and is a convenient way of providing the essential information about the distribution of the random variable.

> To show that a random variable X has a Normal distribution with mean μ and standard deviation σ, you can write
>
> $$X \sim N(\mu, \sigma^2)$$

EXAMPLE 3

The length of life (in months) of a certain hair-drier is approximately Normally distributed with mean 90 months and standard deviation 15.

(a) Each drier is sold with a 5-year guarantee. What proportion of driers fail before the guarantee expires?

(b) The manufacturer decides to change the length of the guarantee so that no more than 1% of driers fail during the guaranteed period. How long should he make the guarantee?

SOLUTION

(a) Let X = length of life of a drier.
Then $X \sim N(90, 15^2)$

5 years is 60 months

$$z = \frac{60 - 90}{15} = -2.0$$

$$P(X < 60) = \Phi(-2.0)$$
$$= 1 - \Phi(2.0)$$
$$= 1 - 0.9772$$
$$= 0.0228$$

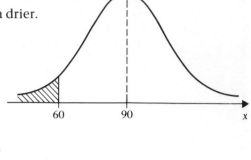

So 2.28% of driers will fail during the guarantee period.

(b)

Let the length of guarantee be t years.

You require $P(X < t) = 0.01$

First find z where $\Phi(z) = 0.01$ $= 1 - 0.99$
$= 1 - \Phi(2.33)$

$\Rightarrow z = -2.33$ (from tables)

$$\Rightarrow -2.33 = \frac{x - 90}{15}$$

$\Rightarrow x = 55.05$ months

90

1%

The manufacturer should give a guarantee of 55 months.

EXERCISE 3

In each of the following questions, assume that the variable is Normally distributed.

1 The mean IQ of a large number of children aged 12 years is 100 and the standard deviation of the distribution is 15. What percentage of children have an IQ of 132 or more?

2 A machine turns out bolts of mean diameter 1.5 cm and standard deviation 0.01 cm. If bolts measuring over 1.52 cm are rejected as oversize, what proportion are rejected in this way?

3 A machine is used to package sugar in 1 kg bags. The standard deviation is 0.0025 kg. To which mean value should the machine be set so that at least 97% of the bags are over 1 kg in mass?

4 Flour is sold in packets marked 1.5 kg. The average mass is 1.53 kg. What should be the maximum value of the standard deviation to ensure that no more than 1 packet in 200 is underweight?

5 An examiner who regularly assigns 10% As, 20% Bs, 40% Cs, 20% Ds and 10% Es sets an examination in which the average mark is 68. The borderline between Cs and Bs is 78. What is the standard deviation?

6 The blood pressures of adult males in England have mean 125 and standard deviation 0. What proportion of the male population has dangerously high blood pressure if the danger level is 140?

7 The mean lifespan for a species of locust is 28 days. If the probability of a locust surviving longer than 31 days is 0.25, estimate the standard deviation of the lifespan.

8 Simply More Pure margarine is sold in tubs with a mean of 500 g and standard deviation 4 g. What proportion of tubs will weigh between 498.5 g and 500.5 g?

9 The heights of girls in a particular year group have mean 154.2 cm and standard deviation 5.1 cm. What percentage of the girls are between 150 cm and 155 cm tall?

10 The results of an examination were Normally distributed. 10% of the candidates had more than 70 marks and 20% had fewer than 35 marks. Find the mean and standard deviation.

After working through this chapter you should:

1 know that, for observations that can be modelled with a Normal distribution, about 68% of all observations lie within ±1 standard deviation of the mean and about 95% are within 2 standard deviations;

2 know how to use tables of the area under the standard Normal curve;

3 know how to solve problems for Normal variables by converting to standardised variables (z-scores) and using approximate (order of magnitude) as well as precise methods;

4 know the notation for a Normal variable X, i.e.

$$X \sim N(\mu, \sigma^2)$$

where μ is the mean value of X and σ is the standard deviation of X.

3 From binomial to Normal

3.1 Binomial to Normal

In *Living with uncertainty* you met the binomial distribution, an important model for a **discrete** random variable under certain conditions. For example, the binomial probability distribution for the number of heads when 35 coins are thrown is shown below.

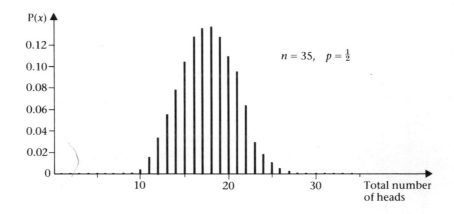

What distribution does this remind you of?

Use the computer program *Binomial* to investigate for what values of n and p you will obtain an approximately bell-shaped curve.

Although there are obvious similarities between some binomial distributions and the Normal curve, there are complications, not least of which is the fact that the Normal distribution models a **continuous** variable, while the binomial distribution is for a **discrete** variable.

What is the difference between a **discrete** and a **continuous** random variable?

3.2 Using the Normal to approximate binomial distributions

In the last section you saw that:

> The binomial distribution is bell-shaped for values of p close to $\frac{1}{2}$, even for quite low values of n.
>
> Even for p not close to $\frac{1}{2}$ the distribution is bell-shaped for larger values of n.

It is difficult to calculate the probabilities of some events using the binomial model.

(a) A box contains 60 dice. A prize of a car is offered to anyone who obtains 30 or more sixes on turning out the dice from the box. Is it worth paying 10p for a turn?

(b) Would it be worth paying 10p if the prize were £10 for 20 or more sixes?

You could, in principle, work out the probabilities of these events using a binomial model, although to do so would be very difficult. It is possible to obtain an approximate result using the Normal distribution as an approximation to the binomial distribution. For example, consider the following situation.

If the probability of being left-handed is found to be 0.1, what is the probability that there will be 60 left-handed children in a school of 500 children?

Let X be the number of left-handed children.
X will have binomial distribution with $p = 0.1$, $n = 500$
It is convenient to write this as:

$$X \sim B(500, 0.1)$$

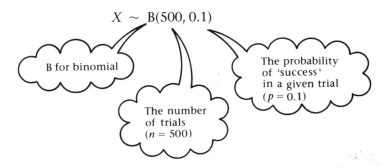

B for binomial

The number of trials $(n = 500)$

The probability of 'success' in a given trial $(p = 0.1)$

The probability of there being **exactly** 60 left-handers is

$$\binom{500}{60} (0.1)^{60} (0.9)^{440}$$

To work out $\binom{500}{60}$ you would need a very large number of rows of Pascal's triangle and the numbers would be too large for a calculator. It would be even more difficult to calculate the probability of 60 **or more**.

$$P(60 \text{ or more}) = P(60) + P(61) + P(62) + \ldots + P(500)$$

The similarity with the Normal distribution may provide an alternative basis for the calculation, since using Normal tables to obtain probabilities is relatively easy.

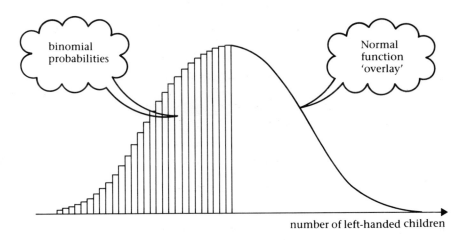

binomial probabilities

Normal function 'overlay'

number of left-handed children

The distribution looks very close to the bell-shaped Normal distribution. In order to obtain the right Normal curve to describe this situation you need to know the mean and variance of the binomial distribution B(500, 0.1).

TASKSHEET 1 — *The mean and variance of the binomial distribution (page 37)*

If a binomial variable is to be modelled by a Normal variable then the Normal variable must have the same mean and the same variance.

The mean of $B(n, p)$ is np.
The variance $B(n, p)$ is $np(1 - p)$.
Since $q = 1 - p$ then $np(1 - p) = npq$.

A binomial model and its Normal approximation should have the same mean and the same variance. If

$$X \sim B(n, p)$$

is approximated by

$$Y \sim N(\mu, \sigma^2)$$

then $\mu = np$, and $\sigma^2 = npq$.

You can use this information to solve the original problem. It can be done approximately as follows.

The number of left-handed children $X \sim B(500, 0.1)$
A Normal variable Y with mean $= np = 50$
and standard deviation $= \sqrt{npq} \approx 6.7$
would model this distribution.

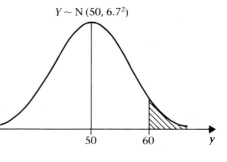

$Y \sim N(50, 6.7^2)$

60 is about $1\frac{1}{2}$ standard deviations above the mean.

i.e. the standardised value is approximately 1.5

$$\Phi(1.5) = 0.9332 \text{ (from tables)}$$

So there is only a 7% probability that there will be more than 60 left-handed children in the school.

Make a similar approximate calculation to show that when 1000 coins are thrown it is likely that between 470 and 530 heads will be obtained.

3.3 More detailed considerations

You have seen that in certain situations, although the binomial distribution really applies it is often more convenient to use the Normal distribution as an approximation. This is particularly true when n is large, when the calculation of binomial probabilities would be very tedious. This approach is illustrated in the following example.

Suppose a student takes a test composed of 48 multiple-choice questions. Each question has 4 possible answers of which only one is correct. The student is unable to answer any of the questions, so she guesses. Find the probability that she will obtain a pass mark by getting 20 or more correct answers.

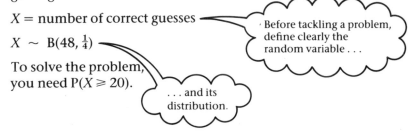

X = number of correct guesses

$X \sim B(48, \frac{1}{4})$

To solve the problem, you need $P(X \geq 20)$.

Before tackling a problem, define clearly the random variable . . .

. . . and its distribution.

What Normal distribution would you use to approximate $B(48, \frac{1}{4})$?

To find the required probability (of 20 **or more** correct guesses) you must take into account the fact that you are using a continuous distribution (Normal) as an approximation to a discrete distribution (binomial). The diagram below shows the right-hand side of the correct binomial distribution.

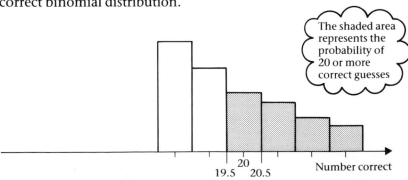

The shaded area represents the probability of 20 or more correct guesses

On the binomial model,
$P(X \geq 20) = P(X = 20) + P(X = 21) + \ldots + P(X = 48)$.
This probability is represented by the shaded columns on the distribution.

You can model the distribution of X (i.e. $B(48, \frac{1}{4})$) with the distribution of a Normal random variable, Y, where $Y \sim N(12, 9)$,

i.e. $Y \sim N(12, 9)$ approximately models $X \sim B(48, \frac{1}{4})$

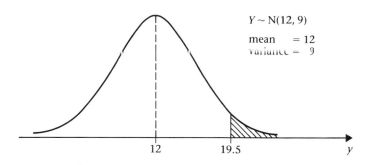

$Y \sim N(12, 9)$

mean $= 12$
variance $= 9$

When $X \sim B(48, \frac{1}{4})$ then $P(X \geqslant 20)$ is approximately the same as $P(Y > 19.5)$ when $Y \sim N(12, 9)$.

The probability for $X \geqslant 20$ is therefore the area to the right of 19.5 on the appropriate Normal distribution. The relevant area is shaded on the diagram above and you can solve the problem using the Normal curve.

The standardised value, z, is given by:

$$z = \frac{y - \mu}{\sigma}$$

For $y = 19.5$

$$z = \frac{19.5 - 12}{3} = 2.5$$

The area to the **left** of z is

$\Phi(2.5) = 0.994$ (to 3 s.f.)

Why is the area to the **right** of $z = 2.5$

$1 - 0.994 = 0.006$?

The probability of a pass using guesswork alone is therefore less than 1%.

33

E X A M P L E   1

Find the probability that between 25 and 30 of the next 50 births at a hospital will be of girls.

S O L U T I O N

Let X = number of girls in 50 births.

You can **assume** that the births of boys and of girls are equally likely.

$X \sim B(50, \frac{1}{2})$ and you need $P(25 < X < 30)$.

> Explain why a binomial distribution is an appropriate model for X.

You need to find $P(25 < X < 30)$

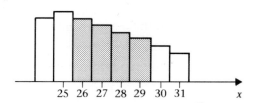

The variable $Y \sim N(25, 3.54^2)$ is an appropriate model for the distribution of X.
You require $P(25.5 < Y < 29.5)$

Standardising $z_1 = \dfrac{29.5 - 25}{3.54} = 1.27$

$z_2 = \dfrac{25.5 - 25}{3.54} = 0.14$

$$
\begin{aligned}
P(25 < X < 30) &= \Phi(1.27) - \Phi(0.14) \\
&= 0.8980 - 0.5557 \\
&= 0.342 \text{ (to 3 s.f.)}
\end{aligned}
$$

EXERCISE 1

1 A coin is tossed a number of times. Using a Normal approximation as appropriate, calculate approximately the probability of:

(a) 52 or more heads in 100 tosses

(b) 520 or more heads in 1000 tosses

(c) 5200 or more heads in 10000 tosses.

2 From experience, an employer finds that he has to reject 30% of applicants as unsatisfactory for employment as machine operatives. What is the probability that after interviewing 200 applicants he will find at least 150 who are suitable for work in his new factory?

3 Thirty dice are thrown. What is the probability of obtaining exactly 5 ones?

4 It is known that 2% of all light bulbs are faulty. What is the probability that there will be more than 20 faulty bulbs in a consignment of 1000?

5 15% of the biscuits produced by a particular machine are misshapen. What is the probability that out of a batch of 1000 biscuits:

(a) fewer than 130 are misshapen;

(b) between 140 and 155 exclusive are misshapen?

6 A gardener sows 75 sunflower seeds in his allotment. The packet states that 80% of the seeds will germinate. What is the probability that more than 65 seeds will germinate?

7 In Eastfork, 24% of the population have blood of type Y. If 250 blood donors are taken at random what is the probability that fewer than 55 will be of blood type Y?

8 A coin is biased so that the probability that it will land heads up is $\frac{3}{5}$. The coin is thrown 160 times. Find the probability that there will be between 90 and 100 heads.

9 In 1984, 11% of households in Britain owned a microwave oven. If a random sample of 200 householders were interviewed, work out the probability that:

(a) fewer than 20 owned a microwave oven;

(b) between 20 and 30 households owned a microwave oven.

10 18.6% of boys and 18.9% of girls leaving school in 1987 had at least one A level.

(a) Calculate the probability of finding, in a random sample of 250 boys who left school in 1987, more than 50 who had at least one A level.

(b) If 300 girls (who left school in 1987) were interviewed, find the probability that between 50 and 60 had at least one A level.

After working through this chapter you should:

1 understand that the Normal distribution can be used as a model for the binomial in some circumstances and that this provides an easy way of estimating binomial probabilities;

2 know that the Normal distribution is a good approximation to $B(n, p)$ if p is close to $\frac{1}{2}$ and that if p is not very close to $\frac{1}{2}$, large values of n are necessary before a Normal distribution can closely fit the particular binomial model;

3 know that if $X \sim B(n, p)$ then mean of $X = np$

   variance of $X = npq$

4 know that if $B(n, p)$ is approximated by $N(\mu, \sigma^2)$, then

$$\mu = np, \qquad \sigma^2 = npq$$

5 be able to use the Normal approximation to the binomial distribution to solve problems.

The mean and variance of the binomial distribution

If a Normal distribution is used as an approximation to a binomial distribution then the Normal and the binomial distributions should have the same mean and variance.

Use the *Binomial* program on the *16–19 Mathematics* statistics computer disc to obtain the mean and variance for a variety of binomial distributions.

1 Copy and complete the table below:

n	p	Mean	Variance
10	$\frac{1}{2}$		
20	$\frac{1}{2}$		
20	$\frac{1}{4}$		
40	$\frac{1}{2}$		
40	$\frac{1}{4}$		
100	$\frac{1}{2}$		

2 Find a formula for the mean in terms of n and p.

3 Find a formula for the variance in terms of n and p.

4 Sampling distribution of the mean

4.1 Sample and population

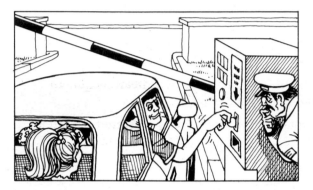

A manufacturer of slot machines decides to check for invalid coins by incorporating a weighing device into each machine. Checking coins is not straightforward since there is considerable variation of the weights of genuine coins. The problem is to decide what **weight range** the machines should accept.

It is not possible to weigh all the coins in circulation in an attempt to find acceptable weight limits. Taking a **sample** of coins is possible but the problem is how to relate information from the sample to the population.

TASKSHEET 1 — Taking samples (page 46)

It is clear that there is a large number of possible samples which may be selected from a population. If, for each sample, the mean is calculated and the distribution of mean values is plotted you obtain the **sampling distribution of the mean**. On tasksheet 1 you should have noticed that:

> The distribution of the sample mean looks like a Normal distribution.
>
> The distribution of the sample mean has the same mean as the parent population.

It is noticeable, however, that the distribution of the sample mean is more tightly clustered around the mean than is the parent population. This is borne out by the fact that its variance is smaller than the variance of the parent population.

4.2 Investigating the sample mean

You will have to explore sample mean distributions further to discover whether the variance of the distribution of the sample mean is related in some way to the variance of the parent population.

TASKSHEET 2 – Coins 2 (page 47)

> The distribution of the sample mean is Normal.
>
> The mean of the distribution of the sample mean is equal to the mean of the parent population.
>
> The larger the sample size the more tightly clustered around its mean is the distribution (i.e. the smaller is the variance of the distribution of the sample mean).
>
> If the population variance is σ^2 and samples of size n are taken, then the distribution of the sample mean of these samples will have variance $\dfrac{\sigma^2}{n}$.

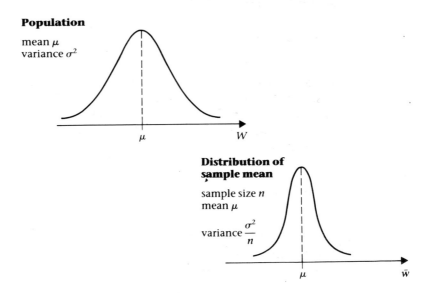

You should now have a good idea of how the distribution of the sample mean is related to that of its parent population.

4.3 From population to sample

It is possible to consider in a little more detail how an acceptable weight interval for a coin machine might be chosen.

Assume that the distribution of all 2p coins in circulation is Normal with mean 7.13 g and variance 0.0061.

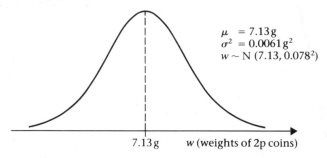

$$\mu = 7.13\,\text{g}$$
$$\sigma^2 = 0.0061\,\text{g}^2$$
$$w \sim N\,(7.13, 0.078^2)$$

7.13 g w (weights of 2p coins)

Suppose the machine accepts 5 coins, each 2p, and records the mean weight.

The distribution of the mean weight of samples of 5 coins will:

- be Normal
- have mean $\mu = 7.13\,\text{g}$
- have variance $\dfrac{\sigma^2}{n} = \dfrac{0.0061}{5}$
  $$= 0.001\,22$$

99.9%

a 7.13 g b 0.0005

0.0005   0.999

$\bar{w}$ (mean weight of 5 coins)

Suppose the acceptance limits a and b are such that the machine accepts 99.9% of all batches of 5 coins.

The limits to include 99.9% of all coins will be very close to 3 standard deviations either side of the mean.

> Check this using Normal tables.

The standard deviation of the distribution of sample means is

$$\sqrt{0.001\,22} = 0.035$$

3.3

Therefore the limits are $7.13 \pm 3 \times 0.035 = 7.13 \pm 0.105$

So the machine should be set to accept batches of coins of mean weight between 7.025 g and 7.235 g.

4.4 Sampling from other distributions

You have been sampling from a parent population which you know is Normal. It is interesting to consider the distribution of the sample mean when other kinds of parent population are sampled.

TASKSHEET 3 — Non-Normal distributions (page 48)

You should have discovered that:

1 The distribution of the sample mean is approximately Normal provided the sample size is large enough, irrespective of the parent population's distribution.

2 The variance of the distribution of the sample mean is the variance of the parent population divided by the sample size. This result is true whatever the size of the sample and whatever the distribution of the parent population.

These important results are known as the **Central Limit Theorem**.

> The Central Limit Theorem states that:
>
> - the distribution of the sample mean is approximately Normal if the sample size is large enough;
>
> - the variance of the distribution of the sample mean is the variance of the parent population divided by the sample size.

The Central Limit Theorem is crucial to work on sampling. It enables you to make predictions about the distribution of the sample mean even if you know nothing about the distribution of the parent population. In addition you can be confident that the mean of the sample is close to the population mean, provided the sample is large enough.

The process of obtaining information about a population based on evidence from a sample is considered in the next chapter.

EXAMPLE 1

The mean weight of trout in a fish farm is 980 g and the standard deviation is 100 g. What is the probability that a catch of 10 trout will have a mean weight per fish of more than 1050 g?

SOLUTION

You can assume that the weight of the population (of all fish in the farm) is N(980, 100^2).

Parent population

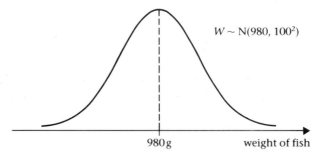

$W \sim N(980, 100^2)$

980 g   weight of fish

The catch of 10 fish is a sample of size $n = 10$. The mean weight of samples of 10:

- is distributed Normally;

- has a mean of 980 g;

- has a variance of $\dfrac{100^2}{10} = 1000 = 31.6^2$.

Distribution of the sample mean
($n = 10$)

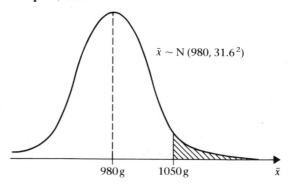

$\bar{x} \sim N(980, 31.6^2)$

980 g   1050 g $\bar{x}$

The probability of obtaining a sample of 10 having a mean weight per fish greater than 1050 g is represented by the shaded area on the sketch of the distribution.

Standardising the weight of 1050 g gives,

$$z = \frac{1050 - 980}{\sqrt{1000}} = 2.21$$

$$P(Z > 2.21) \quad = 1 - \Phi(2.21)$$
$$= 1 - 0.9864 \text{ (from Normal tables)}$$
$$= 0.0136$$

So the probability of obtaining a sample mean weight greater than 1050 g is 0.0136.

i.e. about 1.4% of all samples of 10 will have a mean weight per fish greater than 1050 g.

E X A M P L E 2

Screws are produced with a mean length of 4 cm and standard deviation 0.5 cm. How large a sample should be taken to be 95% certain that the mean of the sample will be within 0.25 cm of the population mean length?

S O L U T I O N

Let the required sample size be n.

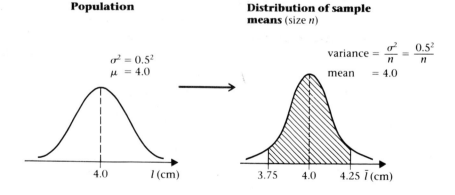

Population

$\sigma^2 = 0.5^2$
$\mu = 4.0$

4.0 l (cm)

Distribution of sample means (size n)

variance $= \dfrac{\sigma^2}{n} = \dfrac{0.5^2}{n}$
mean $= 4.0$

3.75   4.0   4.25 $\bar{l}$ (cm)

So $L \sim N(4.0, 0.5^2)$ and $\bar{L} \sim N\left(4.0, \dfrac{0.5^2}{n}\right)$

You require:

$$P(3.75 < \bar{L} < 4.25) = 0.95$$

This is represented by the shaded area shown.

Consider the upper end of the distribution of sample means.

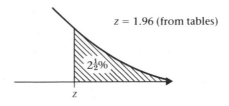

$z = 1.96$ (from tables)

$2\frac{1}{2}\%$

Explain why this value of z is taken.

$$1.96 = \frac{4.25 - 4.0}{0.5/\sqrt{n}}$$

$$\Rightarrow \sqrt{n} = \frac{1.96 \times 0.5}{0.25}$$

$$n = 15.4 \text{ (to 3 s.f.)}$$

To be 95% certain of a sample with mean screw length between 3.75 and 4.25 cm you should take 16 screws.

EXERCISE 1

You may assume that the distributions are Normal.

1 The girls of sixth-form age in a large town have a mean height of 166 cm and standard deviation 6 cm.

In one school there is a mathematics group with 5 girls. What is the probability that the mean height of this group is in the interval (162 cm, 170 cm)?

There are 8 girls in an English group. What is the probability that the mean height of the English group lies in the interval (162 cm, 170 cm)?

2 The mean weight of trout in a fish farm is 980 g. The standard deviation of the weights is 120 g.

See example 1 p 42

If 10 fish are caught at random what is the probability that the mean weight of the catch is in the intervals:

(a) (970 g, 1010 g)   (b) (950 g, 1030 g)   (c) (940 g, 1040 g)?

3 The boys of sixth-form age in a large town have a mean height of 162 cm and standard deviation 3.5 cm.

see example 2 p 43

What size sample of boys must be taken to be 95% certain that the mean height of the sample will be in the intervals:

(a) 160.5 cm to 163.5 cm   (b) 161 cm to 163 cm?

4   The mean weight of 2p coins is 7.3 g. The standard deviation of the weights is 0.078 g.

see example 2

What size sample of coins must be taken to be 95% certain that the mean weight of the sample will be in the intervals:

(a) (7.27 g, 7.33 g)   (b) (7.29 g, 7.31 g)?

5   A packaging machine produces packets of butter with a mean weight of 230 g and standard deviation 5 g. If 10 packets are chosen at random and weighed, what is the probability that they will have a mean weight of more than 253 g?

see example 1

6   The length of a particular species of worm is Normally distributed with mean 5.6 cm and standard deviation 0.4 cm.

(a) What is the probability that a worm chosen at random is longer than 5.7 cm?

(b) Find the probability that the mean length of a sample of 12 worms is greater than 5.7 cm.

After working through this chapter you should:

1   understand that the mean of a sample will have its own distribution, called a **sampling distribution**;

2   know that the distribution of the sample mean is approximately Normal if the sample size is large enough, whatever the nature of the parent population;

3   know that the variance of the distribution of the sample mean is the variance of the parent population divided by the sample size.

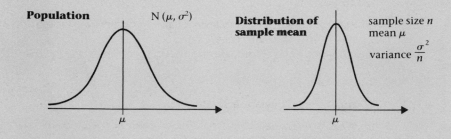

45

Taking samples

You will need:

- The weights of the 100 coins obtained in chapter 1 of this unit

- Recording sheet 2: *Taking samples*

- A computer or calculator that can generate two-digit random numbers (or random number tables)

Weights of 100 2p coins (grams)

7.15	7.08	7.09	7.05	7.33
7.05	7.09	7.12	7.18	7.19
7.08	7.09	7.09	7.20	7.07
7.12	7.11	7.26	6.86	7.14
6.80	7.11	6.99	7.05	7.11
7.27	6.97	7.40	7.12	7.44
7.17	7.17	7.05	7.18	7.13
7.11	7.19	7.16	7.04	7.15
7.11	7.01	7.21	7.02	7.05
7.03	7.22	7.30	7.18	7.14
7.08	7.06	7.30	7.12	7.04
7.11	7.16	7.07	7.22	7.18
7.24	7.20	7.09	7.13	7.11
6.95	7.01	7.18	7.23	7.16
7.00	7.08	7.03	7.04	7.18
7.17	7.12	7.14	7.13	7.18
7.19	7.07	6.98	7.22	7.15
7.34	7.18	7.21	7.06	7.24
6.98	7.25	7.19	7.29	7.17
7.20	7.04	7.17	7.19	7.11

For the weights of coins, you know that the parent population is Normal (or approximately Normal) and its mean and variance are known (mean = 7.13 variance = 0.01).

0.006

1 Use two-figure random numbers to take at least 50 samples of size 2 from the original population. (The coins can be selected more than once.) Calculate the mean of each sample and record your results on recording sheet 2: *Taking samples*.

2 Draw a histogram to illustrate the distribution of the sample means.

3 Calculate the mean and variance of the distribution of the sample mean.

4 Comment on the similarities and differences between the parent population and the distribution of the sample mean.

Coins 2

You will need:

- The computer program *Coins*
- Recording sheet 3: *Coins 2*

Coins enables you to take samples from a data set consisting of the weights of a large number of 2p coins. The population of these coins is Normally distributed, having mean 7.13 and variance 0.006.

1 Choose 400 samples of size 4. Sketch or obtain a printout of the distribution of the sample mean. Record also the mean and variance of the distribution on the recording sheet.

Repeat for samples of size 5, 8, 10 and 20, completing the recording sheet.

2 Describe what happens to the distribution of the sample mean as the sample size increases.

3 Confirm that the mean of the distribution of sample means is equal to that of the population for each different sample size. (As this is an experimental situation you would expect the results to be close, but not exactly equal. If you have any doubts, repeat some of the cases using more samples.)

4 Notice that as sample size increases, the variance of the distribution of sample means decreases. Plot a graph of the variance of the sampling distribution against n (the sample size).

5 Plot a graph of variance against $\dfrac{1}{n}$ and show that it is approximately a straight line through $(0, 0)$.

6 Confirm that the variance of each of the sampling distributions is (approximately) $\dfrac{\sigma^2}{n}$, where σ^2 is the variance of the population of coins.

Non-Normal distributions

You will need:

- The computer program *Dist*
- Recording sheet 4: *Non-Normal distributions*

The computer program *Dist* allows you to enter distributions of your own with which to experiment. You can choose the form of population.

A distribution like this:

x	1	2	3
frequency in millions	1	4	2

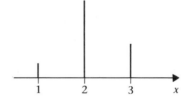

would be entered as follows.

The largest value of x would be given as 3.

The corresponding values of f would be given as 1, 4 and 2.

x	1	2	3
f	1	4	2

The distribution of the chosen population would have four times as many 2s as there are 1s and twice as many 2s as 3s.

| 2 2·2 2   3 3 3 3 3 3 3 3 3

TASKSHEET

3

1 Run the computer program *Dist*.

Choose the largest value of *x* to be 8 and enter the following frequencies:

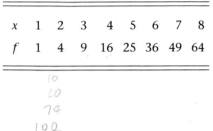

x	1	2	3	4	5	6	7	8
f	1	4	9	16	25	36	49	64

10
20
74
100
204

Choose 200 samples of size 2.

Sketch or obtain print-outs of the distribution of the sample means and of the parent population.

Write on the recording sheet the mean and variance of the distribution of the sample means and of the parent population.

Repeat with samples of size 4, 10, 20, 30, 50.

2 Repeat question 1 with the following distribution

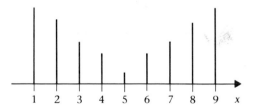

x	1	2	3	4	5	6	7	8	9
f	10	8	6	4	2	4	6	8	10

(a) What can you say about the mean of the sample distributions?

(b) Confirm that the distribution of the sample mean values has a variance of

$$\frac{\sigma^2}{n}$$ approximately.

3 Try to find a distribution where the mean of the sample means is not the same as the mean of the parent population.

Try to find a distribution where the variance of the parent population, the variance of the distribution of the sample means and the sample size are not connected as they were in 1 and 2.

5 Estimating with confidence

5.1 How clean is our water?

Regular checks are made of the water supply to ensure that the degree of pollution is within acceptable limits. One measure of pollution is the degree of acidity, or pH value of the water. Liquids which are 'neutral', that is neither acid nor alkali, have a pH value of 7; a pH value of less than 7 indicates an acid; a pH greater than 7 indicates an alkali. EEC recommendations specify that safe drinking water should have a pH of between 6.5 and 8.5.

In Clean Valley, an environmental group claims that the mean pH is 8.6. Their evidence is based on five random samples of river water.

The members of class 5 from Clean Valley Primary School decide to check the water as part of a pollution project. They collect twenty-five jars of water from the river and calculate a mean pH of 8.5.

The Clean Valley Water Authority, in an effort to clear its name, selects a random sample of one hundred test-tubes of water, and after testing these claims that the mean pH is 8.3.

(a) What justification is there for using the mean pH of a sample as an estimate for the mean pH of Clean Valley's water supply?

(b) Assuming that the scientific method of each group was of the same standard, do you think the water of Clean Valley is safe to drink? Whose evidence would you take most seriously? Discuss your reasons.

Estimating the mean pH of river water is typical of many statistical procedures: you cannot measure the whole population, so you use information from a sample to make estimates of the properties of the population. For example, you might estimate the population mean by using the sample mean.

> An **unbiased estimator** is one for which the mean of its distribution (i.e. the mean of all possible values of the estimator) is equal to the population value it is estimating.
>
> The sample mean is an unbiased estimator of the population mean.

Confidence in how close an estimate is to the actual population mean depends upon the **variability** of the sample mean. For example, suppose you had the evidence of a number of samples, which gave mean values tightly bunched between 7.5 and 8.5, as shown below.

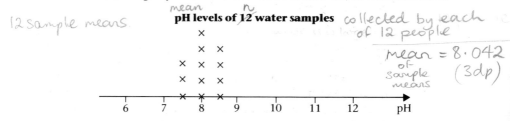

Another batch of samples produced mean values like this:

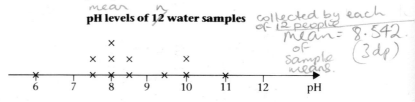

> In which of the two cases would you be more confident of predicting the actual pH level of the water? Why?

Confidence is increased when there is less variation in the sample mean values. This suggests that you might use the variance of the sample mean values as a **measure of confidence**.

In chapter 4 you saw that:

> The variance of the distribution of the sample mean is equal to the variance of the population divided by the sample size
>
> $$\text{variance of } \bar{x} = \frac{\sigma^2}{n}$$

5.2 The standard error

Suppose you know from past experience that the variance of the pH of Clean Valley water is 0.5. Then, for the environmentalists' sample,

$$n = 5, \quad \text{variance of } \bar{x} = \frac{0.5}{n} = 0.1$$

(handwritten: $\bar{X}$ under the fraction)

It is standard practice when reporting an estimate such as this to state the size of the sample and its standard deviation. The standard deviation of $\bar{x}$ is called the **standard error** (s.e.).

(handwritten left margin: $\bar{X}$ ✗ , $\bar{X}$ ✗)

> The standard deviation of the distribution of the sample mean ($\bar{x}$) is called the **standard error** (of the mean).
>
> $$\text{s.e.} = \frac{\sigma}{\sqrt{n}} \qquad = \sqrt{\frac{\sigma^2}{n}}$$

(handwritten: Environmentalists)

For the environmentalists' data:

$$\bar{x} = 8.6 \quad (n = 5, \text{ s.e.} = 0.32)$$

(handwritten: $se = \sqrt{\dfrac{0.5}{5}}$ $[7.48, \; 9.72]$)

(handwritten left: School $8.5(25, 0.141)$ Authority $8.3(100, 0.0707)$)

(handwritten: $[8.01, \; 8.99]$)

> Calculate the standard errors of the other two sample means for Clean Valley water. Write them in $\bar{x}$ (n, s.e.) form, as above.

The smaller the standard error of the sample mean, the less variability you can expect in samples, and so the more confidence you can have in your estimate of the population mean.

(handwritten: $[8.05, \; 8.55]$)

(handwritten: $se = \dfrac{\sigma}{\sqrt{n}} = \sqrt{\dfrac{\sigma^2}{n}}$)

EXERCISE 1 *(handwritten: Population Variance is known.)*

1   Calculate the standard error of the sample mean $\bar{x}$ for a sample of size n from a population of variance σ^2, when

(a) $n = 25, \sigma^2 = 4$ (b) $n = 100, \sigma^2 = 0.9$

2   The following sets of data come from a population whose standard deviation is 2 units. Calculate $\bar{x}$, n and s.e. for each sample.

(a) 6.0, 7.4, 4.3, 4.6, 5.5, 5.6

(b) 7.3, 6.4, 6.5, 6.8, 5.9, 6.7, 5.0, 8.1, 6.5, 5.0, 6.8, 5.2, 5.9, 8.4, 7.7, 7.1, 7.2, 5.8, 8.9, 7.8

(handwritten left: $\mu = 5.7$ $\sigma = 0.5$ $[3.95, 7.45]$ 100% CI)

3   Pure rain falling through clean air is known to have a pH of 5.7 (a little more acidic than most drinking water). Water samples from 40 rainfalls are analysed for pH. The mean pH value of the sample is 3.7. Assuming that the population standard deviation is 0.5, express the result for the sample in $\bar{x}$ (n, s.e.) form. Do you think there is evidence of excess acid in the rain?

(handwritten bottom: $[3.4235, 3.9765]$ 100% CI $3.7\left(40, \dfrac{0.5}{\sqrt{40}}\right) = 3.7(40, 0.079)$)

5.3 Confidence intervals

Stating the size of the sample and the standard error of the mean is one way of expressing how confident you are in your estimate of a population mean, but it is not very 'user-friendly'.

You can express the degree of confidence in your estimate in a more precise way by using an **interval estimate**. The idea is similar to that of tolerance. For example, if a 15 mm panel pin is manufactured to within a tolerance of 1 mm, you could give the length of the pin as

$$15 \, \text{mm} \pm 1 \, \text{mm}$$

meaning that all pins have lengths (in mm) which lie in the interval (14, 16). If about half the pins have lengths within $\frac{1}{2}$ mm of 15 mm, then you could say that the interval (14.5, 15.5) contains about 50% of the population of pins.

You can use the sample mean to construct an interval estimate for the population mean. For example, suppose that in a certain population of adults, height is distributed Normally with a variance of 25 cm². The mean height (μ) is unknown. A random sample of 100 adults has mean height 175 cm. What can you say about the mean height of the whole population of adults?

It is clear that a 'point' estimate of the population mean would have to be 175 cm. However, it would be very unlikely that this **was** the mean. It is better to try to estimate a **range** of possible values which you are confident contains the true value.

You know from earlier work that the mean of samples ($n = 100$) from $N(\mu, \sigma^2)$ will

- be Normally distributed;
- have mean value μ;
- have variance $\dfrac{\sigma^2}{n}$.

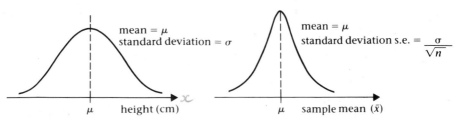

Population distribution　　　　**Sample mean distribution**

mean = μ
standard deviation = σ

μ　　height (cm)

mean = μ
standard deviation s.e. = $\dfrac{\sigma}{\sqrt{n}}$

μ　　sample mean ($\bar{x}$)

Parent Pop^n

Sample Mean

$S = \dfrac{\sigma}{\sqrt{n}}$

You know that 68% of sample mean values are within 1 s.e. of the mean value.

> What evidence do you have for this figure?

When you take a sample, you can be 68% **confident** of getting a value of $\bar{x}$ for the sample which lies in the range: $\mu \pm 1$ s.e.

You can write this as

$$P(\mu - 1 \text{ s.e.} < \bar{x} < \mu + 1 \text{ s.e.}) = 0.68$$

The inequality can be rearranged to give

$$P(\bar{x} - 1 \text{ s.e.} < \mu < \bar{x} + 1 \text{ s.e.}) = 0.68$$

Since 1 s.e. $= \dfrac{\sigma}{\sqrt{n}} = 0.5$ and $\bar{x} = 175\,\text{cm}$ then you are 68% confident that the interval

$$(175 - 0.5) \text{ to } (175 + 0.5) \qquad \text{i.e. } (174.5,\ 175.5)$$

contains the true population mean.

The range of values 174.5 to 175.5 is called a **68% confidence interval for the mean**.

> If you increase your degree of confidence, what happens to the confidence interval?

What proportion of sample means are within 2 standard errors of the true population mean? Calculate another confidence interval which you are much more confident contains the true population mean.

EXAMPLE 1

The water in a particular lake is known to have pH values with variance 0.5^2.

Environmentalists obtain ten samples of water from the lake and test them. The mean pH of the samples is 8.2.

Obtain a 95% confidence interval for the true population mean pH for the lake.

SOLUTION

Approximately 95% of values of $\bar{x}$ lie within 2 s.e. of the true mean (μ).

So $P(\mu - 2\text{ s.e.} < \bar{x} < \mu + 2\text{ s.e.}) = 0.95$
$\Rightarrow P(\bar{x} - 2\text{ s.e.} < \mu < \bar{x} + 2\text{ s.e.}) = 0.95$

Now $\bar{x} = 8.2$, $\quad$ s.e. $= \dfrac{\sigma}{\sqrt{n}} = \dfrac{0.5}{\sqrt{10}} = 0.158$, so

$$8.2 - 2 \times 0.158 < \mu < 8.2 + 2 \times 0.158$$
$$7.88 < \mu < 8.52$$

You can be 95% confident that the interval (7.88, 8.52) contains the population mean μ.

> Calculate a 68% interval and comment on the widths of the 95% and 68% intervals.

EXERCISE 2

1   Children from Clean Valley Primary School collect twenty-five samples of river water. The mean pH of the twenty-five samples is 8.15. The water authority collects one hundred samples with a mean pH of 7.8.

Assume that the variance of pH values for the river is known to be 0.5. Calculate 68% and 95% confidence intervals for the mean pH from:

(a) the primary school results;

(b) the water authority results.

2   Construct a 68% confidence interval and a 95% confidence interval for

(a) a sample with $\bar{x} = 5.57$, $n = 6$, $\sigma = 2$
(b) a sample with $\bar{x} = 6.75$, $n = 20$, $\sigma = 2$

3   What percentage confidence interval is given by calculating $(\bar{x} - 3\text{ s.e.}, \bar{x} + 3\text{ s.e.})$?

5.4 Other intervals

For the Normal distribution, 68% and 95% are approximate figures for confidence given by considering a **whole** number of standard deviations from the sample mean. In practice, confidence intervals are based on 90%, 95% and sometimes 99% confidence. To do this you need to calculate the correct multiple of the standard error which gives these percentages.

TASKSHEET 1 — Confidence intervals (page 65)

You can check the approximate results of tasksheet 1 by calculating areas under the Normal curve.

> Use Normal tables to find z, where $\Phi(z) = 0.95$.

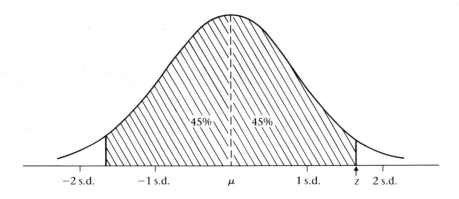

The 90% confidence interval for μ is $(\bar{x} - 1.645 \text{ s.e.}, \bar{x} + 1.645 \text{ s.e.})$

> Show that the **95% confidence interval** for μ is
> $(\bar{x} - 1.96 \text{ s.e.}, \bar{x} + 1.96 \text{ s.e.})$.
>
> Calculate the corresponding 99% confidence interval.

EXERCISE 3

1   A sample of size 9 is drawn from a Normal population with standard deviation 10. The sample mean is 20. Calculate 90%, 95% and 99% confidence intervals for the population mean.

2   Suppose the sample in question 1 were of size 25 (rather than 9). Would the calculated confidence intervals be larger or smaller? Calculate them and verify your prediction.

3   Find a 95% confidence interval for a population mean μ, given a population variance σ^2, sample size n and sample mean $\bar{x}$, where:

(a) $n = 36$ $\bar{x} = 13.1$ $\sigma^2 = 2.42$

(b) $n = 64$ $\bar{x} = 2.65$ $\sigma^2 = 0.234$

(c) $n = 28$ $\bar{x} = 205$ $\sigma^2 = 83.5$

4   Find a 90% confidence interval for a population mean μ given a population variance of σ^2 and a sample of size n with sample mean $\bar{y}$, where:

(a) $n = 125$ $\bar{y} = 0.13$ $\sigma^2 = 0.042$

(b) $n = 60$ $\bar{y} = 20.9$ $\sigma^2 = 3.34$

(c) $n = 55$ $\bar{y} = 845$ $\sigma^2 = 145$

5   A doctor calculates that the mean waiting time for 50 patients is 26 minutes. If the population variance is 6 minutes^2, calculate a 95% confidence interval for waiting times at the surgery.

6   The standard deviation of systolic blood pressure for a population of females is known to be 9.5. The systolic blood pressures of ten women are given below:

   120   134   128   116   120   132   85   98   125   113

Assuming this is a random sample, construct a 90% confidence interval for the mean systolic blood pressure for this population.

7   A random sample of n measurements is selected from a Normal population with unknown mean μ and standard deviation $\sigma = 10$. Calculate the width of a 95% confidence interval for μ when:

(a) $n = 100$ (b) $n = 200$ (c) $n = 400$

Calculate the size of the sample required to give a 95% confidence interval of width 1.

5.5 Estimating a population variance

Suppose that to each member of the world's population you assign −1 if the person is male and +1 if female. Assuming that there are approximately equal numbers of males and females in the world, the distribution of these values has (approximately) $\mu = 0$ and $\sigma^2 = 1$.

> Check that $\sigma^2 = 1$.

A sample of size 2 is shown. The sample mean is 0 and the sample variance is 1.

There are four equally likely samples of size 2:

[male, male], [male, female], [female, male], [female, female]

and so samples of size 2 have the following probability distribution:

Sample	$(-1, -1)$	$(-1, 1)$	$(1, 1)$
Probability	$\frac{1}{4}$	$\frac{1}{2}$	$\frac{1}{4}$
Sample mean, $\bar{x}$	-1	0	1
Sample variance	0	1	0

(handwritten margin notes)

-1-1-1 -1-11 -1 11 111
1/8 3/8 3/8 1/8
-1 -1/3 1/3 1
0 8/9 8/9 0

1 → Mean = 0

Mean
Sample variance = 0×

> Explain the entries in the table above.
>
> Calculate a similar table for samples of size 3.
>
> For both $n = 2$ and $n = 3$, explain how your results illustrate the fact that $\bar{x}$ is an unbiased estimator of μ.

(handwritten at bottom)
Mean sample variance $= \frac{1}{8} \times 0 + \frac{1}{8} \times 0 + \frac{3}{8} \times \frac{8}{9} + \frac{3}{8} \times \frac{8}{9} = \frac{2}{3}$

(handwritten margin notes)

$n = 4$

les 4 3 2 1 0

b $\frac{1}{16}$ $\frac{4}{16}$ $\frac{6}{16}$ $\frac{4}{16}$ $\frac{1}{16}$

-1 $-\frac{1}{2}$ 0 $\frac{1}{2}$ 1 → mean = 0

0 $\frac{3}{4}$ 1 $\frac{3}{4}$ 0

x	$(x-\bar{x})^2$		x	$(x-\bar{x})^2$
-1	0·25		-1	1
-1	2·25		-1	1
-1	0·25			1
1	2·25		1	1
	3·00			4

ean of sample variances

$\frac{1}{16} \times 0 + \frac{4}{16} \times \frac{3}{4} + \frac{6}{16} \times 1$

$+ \frac{4}{16} \times \frac{3}{4} + \frac{1}{16} \times 0$ (mean)

$\frac{3}{16} + \frac{6}{16} + \frac{3}{16}$

$\frac{12}{16}$

$= \frac{3}{4}$

The distribution of the sample variances is as shown.

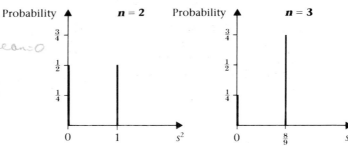

Although the population variance is 1, these distributions have means of $\frac{1}{2}$ and $\frac{2}{3}$ respectively.

> When $n = 3$, show that the mean of the distribution of sample variances is $\frac{2}{3}$.

Unlike the distribution of sample means, the mean of the distribution of sample variances does **not** equal the population variance. So the sample variance is not an unbiased estimator of population variance.

> The sample variance is a **biased** estimator of the population variance.

It is straightforward (but perhaps tedious) to repeat the calculations of this section for samples of size 4, 5, 6, . . . The results are striking:

n	2	3	4	5	6	7	. . .
Mean of the distribution of s^2	$\frac{1}{2}$	$\frac{2}{3}$	$\frac{3}{4}$	$\frac{4}{5}$	$\frac{5}{6}$	$\frac{6}{7}$	. . .

As the sample size increases, s^2 looks increasingly good as an estimator for σ^2 (which is equal to 1). However, for small n, it looks as if you should use $\left(\dfrac{n}{n-1} \right) s^2$ as an estimator for σ^2.

Remarkably, this result holds generally, not just for the special distribution considered in this section.

> If s^2 is the sample variance of a sample of size n then
>
> $\left(\dfrac{n}{n-1} \right) s^2$ is an unbiased estimator of the population variance.

The quantity $\left(\dfrac{n}{n-1}\right)s^2$ is obtained on many calculators by pressing the σ_{n-1} key (instead of σ_n) and then squaring. For large samples, the difference between σ_{n-1} and σ_n is small and usually masked by the fact that s^2 varies considerably.

A rigorous demonstration that $\left(\dfrac{n}{n-1}\right)s^2$ is an unbiased estimator of σ^2 is beyond the scope of this unit. The result is studied further on tasksheet 2E.

TASKSHEET 2E – Boxes of matches (page 66)

EXERCISE 4

1 Use the relevant formulas and the statistical functions on your calculator to calculate the sample variance and $\left(\dfrac{n}{n-1}\right)s^2$ for each of the following samples

(a) the heights of eight students in metres: 1.54, 1.66, 1.62, 1.68, 1.65, 1.63, 1.67, 1.65;

(b) the speeds of ten cars entering a village in $\mathrm{km\,h}^{-1}$: 45, 40, 49, 53, 48, 57, 50, 60, 47, 56.

2 Calculate s^2 for each of the following samples. Hence write down an estimate of the population variance.

(a) The sizes of men's shoes sold in one week in a shoe shop:

Size	39	40	41	42	43	44	45	46
Pairs sold	1	6	13	20	25	14	7	1

(b) The lifetimes in minutes of twenty batteries:

Lifetime (min)	0–60	61–90	91–120	121–150	151–180	181–210	211–240
Number of batteries	1	0	1	5	7	4	2

3 An inspector of weights and measures selects at random six bags of flour from a consignment and finds the weights in kilograms to be 1.502, 1.499, 1.506, 1.497, 1.501, 1.503. Find unbiased estimates for the mean and variance of the weights of the bags in this entire consignment of flour.

5.6 Populations with unknown variance

So far, to calculate confidence intervals, you have assumed:

- that you know the standard deviation of the population (so that you can work out the standard error of the sample mean).

- that the distribution of the sample mean is Normal.

> Are these reasonable assumptions? What can you do if they are not?

Suppose you conduct clinical trials for a drug company and are testing a drug to see how effective it is. For 29 patients with the same disease, you measure the remission time (the number of days' relief from symptoms after taking the drug). These remission times in days are as follows:

> 5, 12, 7, 24, 1, 23, 20, 23, 15, 20, 5, 13, 15, 16, 9, 2, 13, 34, 21, 19, 12, 2, 13, 12, 10, 3, 4, 6, 35

(a) From these data, can you calculate the standard error of the mean remission time?

(b) Do you know the population standard deviation in this case? What could you use instead?

(c) Do you think the distribution of remission time is likely to be Normal? Is the distribution of **mean** remission time Normal?

The population variance is often not known when calculating confidence intervals from samples. In this case you can use the sample standard deviation to estimate the population standard deviation.

You will recall that there are **two** possible estimators for the population variance: the sample variance itself, s^2, and $\dfrac{ns^2}{(n-1)}$.

There is a variety of notations for these values. It is conventional to denote them by $s_n{}^2$ and $s_{n-1}{}^2$, respectively.

s_n^2 is the variance of the sample of n data values.

$s_{n-1}^2 = \dfrac{n}{n-1} s_n^2$ is an unbiased estimator for σ^2.

s_n^2 is biased, whereas s_{n-1}^2 is unbiased. However, when n is large, the difference between these two estimators becomes insignificant and for large samples (for example $n > 25$) you can use the variance of the sample as your estimate of the population variance.

For the remission data above, calculate 95% confidence limits for the population mean, using (i) s_n^2, (ii) s_{n-1}^2 as an estimator for the population variance.

Throughout this unit, s_{n-1}^2 is used to estimate the population variance, on the grounds that it is unbiased.

EXAMPLE 2

A random sample of 15 visitors to the York Viking Museum showed that they had waited the following times (in minutes) to get in:

19, 28, 34, 10, 27, 31, 25, 37, 54, 27, 54, 8, 17, 24, 21

Estimate a 95% confidence interval for the mean waiting time.

SOLUTION

Working in minutes, the sample has mean 27.73.
The variance of the sample values is 165.3.
An unbiased estimate of the population variance (s_{n-1}^2)
is $\dfrac{15}{14} \times 165.3 = 177.1$

An estimate of the standard error is $\dfrac{\sqrt{177.1}}{\sqrt{15}} = 3.44$

The 95% confidence interval for waiting times is 27.73 ± 1.96 s.e. minutes, i.e. (21.0, 34.5) minutes.

On tasksheet 3 the assumption that the distribution of the sample mean is Normal is investigated.

TASKSHEET 3 — Another distribution (page 69)

When the background population is **not** Normal, the distribution of the sample mean becomes more and more nearly Normal for larger and larger samples. You have met this idea before as the Central Limit Theorem.

EXERCISE 5

1 Calculate an approximate 95% confidence interval for the population mean using the following sample data:

(a) $n = 36$, $\bar{x} = 10$, sample variance = 4

(b) $n = 100$, $\bar{x} = 20$, sample variance = 9

(c) $n = 5$, $\bar{x} = 20$, $s_n^2 = 0.01$

Give a reason why your answer to part (c) may be unreliable.

2 In an alpine skiing competition, the times taken by the 59 competitors to complete the course gave a mean of 1 minute 54 seconds. The standard deviation of the sample was 4.1 seconds. Calculate a 90% confidence interval for the mean time to complete the course.

3 A population of small fish was sampled, giving the following age distribution:

Age (years)	1	2	3	4	5	6	7	8	9
Frequency	0	80	345	243	124	56	34	6	3

Find an approximate 95% confidence interval for the mean age of this population of fish. Write down in your own words how you would explain the meaning of this interval to a local fisherman not versed in the art of statistics.

4 (a) Calculate a 90% confidence interval for the population mean based on a sample with $n = 10$, $\bar{x} = 10$ and $s_n = 4$.

(b) Why is the interval not reliable in this case?

After working through this chapter you should:

1   appreciate that any statistic taken from a sample will have its own distribution and may be used to estimate measures for the whole population;

2   know what the terms biased and unbiased estimators mean;

3   know that the sample mean is an unbiased estimator of the population mean;

4   know that, for a sample size n, the sample variance s^2 is a biased estimator of the population variance but $\dfrac{ns^2}{n-1}$ is unbiased;

5   understand that the standard error of the sample mean gives a measure of how close the sample mean is likely to be to the population mean;

6   understand the idea of a confidence interval for the population mean, and be able to construct 90%, 95% and 99% confidence intervals from a sample of a population with known variance;

7   know how and when it is appropriate to construct confidence intervals for the mean of a population when the variance is not necessarily known, using a large sample.

Confidence intervals

You will need:
- The computer program   *Conf*

This is a computer simulation of confidence intervals.

Run the computer program *Conf*, which generates samples of size n from a Normal population $N(\mu, \sigma^2)$. From each sample it constructs a confidence interval for μ of the form $(m - ks, m + ks)$ where s is the standard error and k is a constant. The number of intervals which contain μ is then counted and the first five intervals are displayed on the screen.

Run the program for various values of μ, σ and n.

(a) Take 1000 samples and use trial and improvement to find the value of k (to 1 d.p.) which gives a 90% confidence interval (that is, about 90% of samples contain μ).

(b) Find the percentage confidence interval produced by using $k = 1.96$.

```
          S.M.P. - CONF

   Enter Mean µ of distribution ?1
   Enter standard deviation σ ?0.2
   Enter sample size n (2<n<25) ?10
   Enter number of samples N ?1000

   Enter a value for k ?1.9

        The first five intervals are:

                ( 0.877 , 1.117 )
                ( 0.828 , 1.069 )
                ( 0.896 , 1.137 )
                ( 0.831 , 1.071 )
                ( 0.735 , 0.976 )

   Intervals containing mean: 935
   Intervals tested so far: 1000

   k = 1.9    Standard error = 6.32E-2
   Percentage confidence interval = 93.5%

   Press K to change value of k.
   Press ESCAPE to restart.
```

Boxes of matches

2E

Boxes of matches often have on the side a statement such as:

Suppose you want to check whether this is true and find out more information about the distribution of the number of matches in a box. The obvious thing to do is to take a random sample of perhaps 1000 matchboxes and count the matches in each. You could then work out the average number of matches in a box and the standard deviation of the number of matches. You could get some idea of the shape of the population distribution by drawing a frequency diagram for your sample of 1000 boxes. This would take a good deal of time and you might find you could only deal practically with a very much smaller number of matchboxes; so it would be useful to see what information can be obtained from much smaller samples.

Taking the problem to its opposite extreme, consider what information could be obtained from a sample of size 2, just two matchboxes, whose contents are counted. Suppose that one box contained 47 matches and the other contained 48 matches. The sample of two boxes has a mean of 47.5 and you can work out the variance as 0.25. To see what can be inferred from this sample you can look at the problem the other way round and assume that you know what the population looks like (its distribution, mean and variance). You can then investigate possible samples of size 2.

Use a simple model for the population: assume that 20% of boxes contain 47 matches, 60% contain 48 matches and 20% contain 49 matches.

x	47	48	49
$P(X = x)$	0.2	0.6	0.2

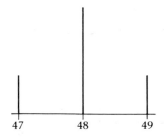

1 Show that the population mean is 48 and that the population variance is 0.4.

If a random sample of two boxes is chosen from the population, then there are just 9 possibilities.

> A sample of 48, 49 has probability 0.12

Probabilities

	47	48	49
47	0.04	0.12	0.04
48	0.12	0.36	0.12
49	0.04	0.12	0.04

Values of $\bar{x}$

	47	48	49
47	47.0	47.5	48.0
48	47.5	48.0	48.5
49	48.0	48.5	49.0

Values of s^2

	47	48	49
47	0.00	0.25	1.00
48	0.25	0.00	0.25
49	1.00	0.25	0.00

2 Show that the probability of obtaining a sample having $\bar{x} = 48.5$ is 0.24.

Both $\bar{x}$ and s^2 have distributions:

Sample mean $\bar{x}$

$\bar{x}$	47.0	47.5	48.0	48.5	49.0
$P(\bar{X} = x)$	0.04	0.24	0.44	0.24	0.04

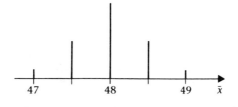

Sample variance s^2

y	0	0.25	1
$P(s^2 = y)$	0.44	0.48	0.08

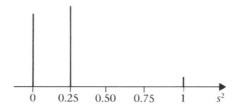

The original distribution was symmetrical. Note that $\bar{x}$ has a symmetrical distribution, but that s^2 does not.

3 (a) Show that the mean value of the distribution of $\bar{x}$ is 48.

   (b) Show that the mean value of the distribution of s^2 is 0.2.

Comparing these values with $\mu = 48$ and $\sigma^2 = 0.4$, you can see that if you took a large number of samples of size 2, the distribution of their means ($\bar{x}$) would be symmetrical and have mean value μ; but the distribution of their variance (s^2) would have a mean value of only $\frac{1}{2}\sigma^2$.

4 Investigate taking samples of size 2 from other populations of matches:

Rectangular

x	47	48	49
$P(X = x)$	$\frac{1}{3}$	$\frac{1}{3}$	$\frac{1}{3}$

$\bar{x} = \text{Mean} = 48 \qquad s^2 = 2/3$

U-shaped

$\mu = 48 \qquad \sigma^2 = 2 \times \frac{2}{3} = \frac{4}{3}$

x	47	48	49
$P(X = x)$	0.5	0	0.5

$\bar{x} = 48 \qquad s^2 = 1$

Asymmetrical

x	47	48	49
$P(X = x)$	0.6	0.3	0.1

$\bar{x} = 47.5$

2256.7
2256.25

$s^2 = 0.45$

$\mu = 47.5$

$\sigma^2 = \frac{9}{10}$

$= \frac{45}{100} = \frac{9}{20}$

$\mu = 48 \qquad \sigma^2 = 2$

Comment on your findings and produce unbiased estimates for the mean and variance of the population from which the original sample of two boxes was drawn.

You could use a computer simulation to investigate samples of size other than 2.

Another distribution

You will need:
● The computer program – *Conf 2*

The program *Conf 2* is similar to *Conf*, except that it samples from what is called a **rectangular distribution**.

A rectangular distribution

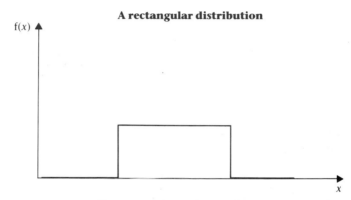

The distribution is symmetrical but certainly not Normal.

Conf 2 takes samples of 25 random numbers in the range 0–10. It also uses the sample variance as an estimate of the population variance and calculates a standard error from this estimate.

Run the program, taking $N = 500$ and $k = 1.96$, then $k = 1.64$. Check that this gives approximate 95% and 90% confidence intervals.

```
         S.M.P.  -  C O N F 2

 Size of samples = 25
 Enter number of samples N ?500
 Enter a value for k ?1.96

      The first five intervals are:

          ( 4.0883 , 6.1429 )
          ( 4.4602 , 6.6138 )
          ( 4.8030 , 7.0685 )
          ( 4.9536 , 6.5959 )
          ( 3.8961 , 6.1665 )

 Intervals containing mean: 472
 Intervals tested so far: 500

              k = 1.96
 Percentage confidence interval = 94.4%

       Press ESCAPE to restart.
```

 **Population proportions**

6.1 How many are there?

Suppose a biologist wants to find out how many fish there are in a lake.

One commonly-used method is the 'capture–recapture' technique. The biologist catches a number of the fish, for example 50, marks them in some way, and puts them back into the lake. Some time later she catches a batch of 40 fish and observes how many of them are marked.

 If 5 of the 40 fish caught are marked, what should be her estimate of the total number of fish in the lake? $8 \times 50 = 400$

How accurate do you think this estimate will be?

 TASKSHEET 1 — Sampling fish (page 76)

It is likely that your estimates for the total number of fish were not very accurate. The variability in using the single sample as an estimate may be overcome if you use the mean value of several sample estimates.

Suppose there are N fish in the lake and you wish to **estimate** N. To do this you can first catch and mark a known number of fish n, releasing them back into the lake. The proportion of **marked** fish in the lake is then $\dfrac{n}{N}$.

After a period of time, suppose a second catch (for example of 50 fish) contains x marked fish. Then the proportion of marked fish in the catch is $\dfrac{x}{50}$.

$$\frac{x}{50} = \frac{n}{N} \Rightarrow N = \frac{50n}{x}$$

> Explain why the estimated number of fish in the lake is $\dfrac{50n}{x}$.

The quantity $\dfrac{50n}{x}$ is an **estimator** of the number of fish in the lake. As you have seen, it varies (considerably in this case) from sample to sample, having its own distribution with some values being more probable than others.

Since it is possible for x to be zero, the mean value of the distribution of $\dfrac{50n}{x}$ is infinite. In this case the estimator does **not** average out to the population value and so $\dfrac{50n}{x}$ is a **biased estimator** for the number of fish in the lake.

In practice, the biologist would normally have only one sample measurement to work with and would use this estimator, despite its bias.

6.2 Opinion polls

One important area of application of some of the ideas encountered in this unit is that of trying to find out how the population would vote in an election. Newspapers and television companies often engage professional organisations (such as Mori or Gallup) to conduct an opinion poll for them. The poll is of a carefully selected random sample of the population. Your earlier work has been about obtaining information on a population mean from a sample. Most opinion polls set out to tackle another problem – what **proportion** (or percentage) of the population will vote for a particular party.

For example, suppose that a survey of 400 randomly selected adults shows that 144 will vote Conservative at the next general election. To obtain a 95% confidence limit for the proportion of the population which will vote Conservative, you can proceed as follows:

Let p be the proportion of the population who will vote Conservative. Although p is not known, an estimate would be $\frac{144}{400} = 0.36$. You need a confidence interval for this estimate.

Let X be the number of people in a sample who will vote Conservative. Then $X \sim B(400, p)$.

> Explain why X has this distribution.

Mean $(X) = np = 400p$
Variance $(X) = np(1 - p) = 400p(1 - p)$

For large samples ($n = 400$ here) you can approximate this distribution with a Normal distribution having the same mean and variance. So:

$$X \sim N(400p, 400p(1 - p))$$

For 95% of samples,

$$400p - 1.96 \sqrt{400p(1 - p)} < X < 400p + 1.96 \sqrt{400p(1 - p)} \quad ①$$

$$\frac{X}{400} - 1.96 \sqrt{\frac{p(1 - p)}{400}} < p < \frac{X}{400} + 1.96 \sqrt{\frac{p(1 - p)}{400}} \quad ②$$

Handwritten annotations on left margin:

$X < 400p + 1.96\sqrt{}$

$\dfrac{X}{400} < p + \dfrac{1.96\sqrt{}}{400}$

$\Rightarrow \dfrac{X}{400} - 1.96 \sqrt{\dfrac{400p(1-p)}{400^2}}$

$> \dfrac{X}{400} - 1.96 \sqrt{\dfrac{p(1-p)}{400}}$

> Carefully show how inequality ② can be deduced from inequality ①.

The interval you have obtained is the 95% confidence interval for p, the proportion of the population which will vote Conservative.

Unfortunately, the expression cannot be evaluated as you cannot

work out $\sqrt{\dfrac{p(1 - p)}{400}}$ because p is not known! Since you have

a large sample, however, you can take the sample value $\dfrac{X}{400} = 0.36$ as

an estimate of p. So, approximately,

$$0.36 - 1.96 \sqrt{\frac{0.36 \times 0.64}{400}} < p < 0.36 + 1.96 \sqrt{\frac{0.36 \times 0.64}{400}}$$

You can be 95% confident that between 31.3% and 40.7% of the population will vote Conservative. In general:

> If p_s is the proportion in a sample of size n, the 95% confidence interval for the population proportion, p, is
>
> $$p_s - 1.96 \sqrt{\frac{p_s(1 - p_s)}{n}} < p < p_s + 1.96 \sqrt{\frac{p_s(1 - p_s)}{n}}$$

TASKSHEET 2 — Opinion polls (page 77)

EXAMPLE 1

A school of 300 pupils has 42 who are left-handed. Obtain a 95% confidence interval for the proportion of the population (p) who are left-handed.

SOLUTION

The proportion of left-handed pupils in the school $= \dfrac{42}{300} = 0.14$

A 95% confidence interval for the population proportion (p) is

$$0.14 - 1.96 \sqrt{\frac{0.14 \times 0.86}{300}} < p < 0.14 + 1.96 \sqrt{\frac{0.14 \times 0.86}{300}}$$

$$0.10 < p < 0.18 \text{ (to 2 s.f.)} \qquad \text{i.e. between 10% and 18%.}$$

EXERCISE 1

1   The newspaper cutting shows the results of a poll of 750 travellers on British Rail following a bomb scare at a London main-line station.

BRITISH RAIL closed all the London mainline stations for several hours this week following a bomb scare and urged London's half a million commuters to stay at home. Commuters were asked:

	Total (750)	Male (444)	Female (306)	18-34 (313)	35+ (437)
Should they have done this? YES	69%	67%	72%	77%	64%
Or should they have publicised the warning, kept the stations open and allowed the public to make their own decisions? YES	25	27	22	19	29
Don't know	6	7	6	4	7

Evening Standard

(a) Calculate 95% confidence limits for the proportion of

(i) male   (ii) female

travellers who felt British Rail were correct in advising passengers to stay at home.

(b) Calculate a 90% confidence interval for the proportion of 18–34 year-olds who felt they should have let passengers make up their own minds.

$p_s = \dfrac{12}{30} = 0.4$

2 A biologist marks 50 fish in a lake. Two days later she returns and catches 30 fish, 12 of which are marked.

(a) Calculate a 95% confidence interval for the proportion of marked fish in the lake.

(b) Hence work out a 95% confidence estimate for the number of fish in the lake.

3 A local council conducts a quick poll and discovers that about 50% of people would support a new shopping complex. In order to estimate this proportion more accurately (to within ± 2%) it decides to have a second poll of size n. Calculate n for:

(a) 90% confidence   (b) 95% confidence

After working through this chapter you should:

1   be able to calculate approximate confidence intervals for a population proportion based on a large sample;

2   know that, if the proportion in a sample of size n is p_s then a 95% confidence interval for the population proportion is:

$$\left(p_s - 1.96 \sqrt{\frac{p_s(1 - p_s)}{n}} , p_s + 1.96 \sqrt{\frac{p_s(1 - p_s)}{n}} \right)$$

Sampling fish

You will need:
- A bag
- About 300 white tiles and 50 coloured tiles

This experiment simulates the capture–recapture method for a population of unknown size. Your task is to estimate the number of tiles in a bag using capture–recapture.

You need a bag of white tiles (an unknown number but somewhere in the region of 200–300). Replace 50 of the white tiles with coloured tiles.

Select a sample of 25 tiles from the bag and count how many of them are coloured.

What proportion of your sample is coloured?

What is your estimate of the number of tiles in the bag?

Repeat the experiment about 20 times (keeping the same number of tiles in the bag). Record each estimate. Empty the bag and count the total number of tiles that it contains.

Calculate the average of your estimates.

How good a method do you think this is?

Give a reason for your answer.

Opinion polls

The extract is from an article in the *Daily Telegraph*: 11 August 1989. Read the article and answer the questions.

GALLUP 9000

THE PARTIES

If there were a General Election tomorrow, which party would you support?

	1987 Election	May '89	June '89	July '89	Change since June	Latest
Lab	31.5	40.8	41.3	43.3	+2.0	44½
Con	43.3	40.9	38.2	35.5	−2.7	34
Green	0.4	2.6	6.4	8.6	+2.2	9
Dems	23.1	8.8	7.3	6.9	−0.4	5½
SDP	–	4.0	3.7	3.1	−0.6	4½
Other	1.7	2.8	3.0	2.5	−0.5	2½

THE GOVERNMENT

Do you approve or disapprove of the Government's record to date?

	June	July	Change
Approve	32.8	29.9	−2.9
Disapprove	54.3	57.6	+3.3

THE LEADERS

Are you satisfied or dissatisfied with Mrs Thatcher as Prime Minister?

	June	July	Change
Satisfied	37.7	34.8	−2.9
Dissat'fied	56.8	60.1	+3.3

Do you think Mr Kinnock is or is not proving a good leader of the Labour Party?

	June	July	Change
Is.................	37.5	37.9	+0.4
Is not..........	50.3	49.9	−0.4

Do you think Mr Ashdown is or is not proving a good leader of the Social and Liberal Democrats?

	June	July	Change
Is.................	25.7	21.7	−4.0
Is not..........	39.6	44.4	+4.8

The July Gallup 9000 is based on 9,502 interviews conducted face-to-face between July 1 and July 31 in more than 350 districts across Great Britain. The figures in the column headed "Latest" in the voting-intention table are based on a sample of 924 electors interviewed between August 2 and August 7 in 100 districts across the country.

The Gallup 9000 sample is large enough that its findings can be reported to one decimal place. In the case of the smaller "snapshot" survey, the findings are rounded to the nearest whole or half number. The "don't knows", excluded from the latest voting figures, amount to 8 per cent.

The sample was based on 9502 interviews.

1   Calculate a 95% confidence interval for the proportion of the population who are satisfied with:

(a) Mrs Thatcher   (b) Mr Kinnock

2   43.3% said they would vote Labour. Calculate a 90% confidence interval for the population proportion.

3   The 'latest' figures are based on a sample of only 924 people. 44½% said they would vote Labour. Find a 99% confidence interval for the population proportion who will vote Labour.

4E   The author states that for the Gallup 9000 poll it is acceptable to report the percentages correct to 1 decimal place. Confirm that this is so.

Solutions

1 An important distribution

1.3 Standardising the data

> Debbie scored 64 for mathematics and 78 for economics.
>
> Which was the better result?

You cannot say which was the better result without some other information, such as the spread of marks. Although her score in economics is higher, everyone may have scored highly in economics, whereas her mathematics result might have been among the best in the class.

> The mean and standard deviation of the standardised scores are approximately 0 and 1 respectively for this data set.
>
> Investigate other small data sets and comment on your findings.

Other data sets will produce the same results for the mean and the standard deviation. In each case the mean of standardised data is 0 and the standard deviation is 1, although rounding errors in the calculations will lead only approximately to these values.

EXERCISE 1

1   (a) -1 (b) -2.833 (c) 1   (d) $\dfrac{x - m}{d}$

2   (a)

	Standardised scores	
	Mathematics	Economics
Karen	0.833	0.375
Alex	-2.708	-3.375
Melanie	0	0
Chris	-7.083	-5.375

(b) Mathematics 64 (2.08 standardised):   Economics $\dfrac{x - 68}{8} = 2.08 \Rightarrow x \approx 85$

(c) $\dfrac{x - 54}{4.8} = \dfrac{x - 68}{8} \Rightarrow x = 33$

3 (a) The man is relatively taller.

Male: $\dfrac{-1}{2.8} = -0.36$;   Female: $\dfrac{-1}{2.4} = -0.42$

(b) 5 ft 9 in.

1.4 Considering the area

> What does the **area** of each block represent?
>
> What does the total area of all the blocks represent?

The area of each block represents frequency in the corresponding interval, i.e. 8, 29, 46, 12 and 5. The total area of all the blocks represents the frequency or total number of values, i.e. 100.

The area of a frequency density histogram is dependent on the total frequency. Since this is different in each case, each histogram will have a different area.

> What is the total relative frequency?
>
> What is the total area of the histogram?
>
> Draw the relative frequency density histogram for one of the data sets A–E from datasheet 1. Confirm that the total area is 1.

The total relative frequency is 1 and will always be so for any data set.

The area of each block is:

height of block × width = relative frequency for the block

The total area of the histogram is the sum of the areas of the separate blocks, which is the same as the sum of the relative frequencies. The area of a relative frequency density histogram is therefore 1.

The relative frequency density histograms will be similar to those you obtained on tasksheet 2 but with different vertical scales. For example:

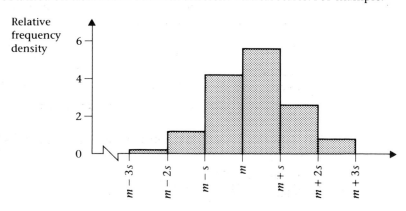

1.5   The 'Normal' curve

> Describe the shape and area properties of the Standard Normal curve.

The curve is symmetrical about the mean, 0, and the area under the curve is equal to 1. About $\frac{2}{3}$ of all observations are within 1 standard deviation of the mean. About 95% of all observations are within 2 standard deviations. Observations more than 3 standard deviations from the mean are very unlikely.

2   The Normal distribution

2.1   Introduction

> Use your knowledge of areas under the Normal curve to find the proportion of eggs having weights between 60 g and 75 g.

If approximately 70% of the weights lie within ± 1 standard deviation of the mean, then by using the symmetry property of the curve, approximately 35% of the weights will lie between the mean (60 g) and +1 standard deviation (75 g).

2.2   Area and probability

EXERCISE 1

1   Your values should be, approximately:

a	b	Area
0	1	0.341
1	2	0.136
2	3	0.0215

2   The area between ± 1 s.d. is 0.682.

The area between ± 2 s.d. is 0.954.

The area between ± 3 s.d. is 0.997.

3   (a) 0.68   (b) 0.046   (c) 0.001

2.3 Tables for the Normal function

Using this information alone, what other areas can you find?

$$P(z > 2) = 0.023$$
$$P(0 < z < 2) = 0.477$$
$$P(-2 < z < 0) = 0.477$$
$$P(z < -2) = 0.023$$
$$P(-2 < z < 2) = 0.954$$
$$P(|z| > 2) = 0.046 \quad \text{etc.}$$

EXERCISE 2

1 (a) 0.092

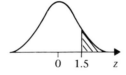

(b) (i) 0.067   (ii) 0.977

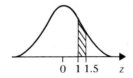   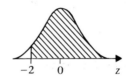

(c) (i) 0.947   (ii) 0.929   (iii) 0.055

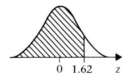   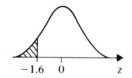

(d) (i) 0.045   (ii) 0.775   (iii) 0.242

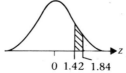      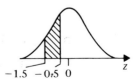

2 (a) 0.683   (b) 0.954   (c) 0.997

3 (a) $z = 1.22$

(b) $z = 0.44$

(c) $z = 1.50$

(d) $z = -0.04$

(e) $z = -1.15$

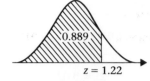

4 (a) $z = -1.52$

(b) $z = -1.18$

(c) $z = 0.77$

(d) $z = 0.35$

(e) $z = -0.07$

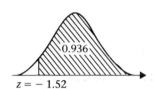

2.4 Normal distributions

> Approximately what proportion of women will have a height greater than 166 cm?

As 166 cm is approximately 1 standard deviation above the mean, you could expect approximately 16% of women to have a height greater than 166 cm.

E X E R C I S E 3

1 $z = \dfrac{132 - 100}{15} = 2.133$ $\Phi(2.133) = 0.983$ (to 3 s.f.)

The percentage with an IQ of 132 or more is 1.7%.

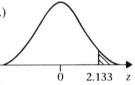

2 $z = \dfrac{1.52 - 1.5}{0.01} = 2$ $\Phi(2) = 0.9772$

The proportion rejected as being over 1.52 cm is 2.3%.

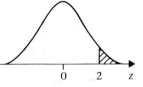

3 $\Phi(z) = 0.97$ $z = -1.88$

$-1.88 = \dfrac{1 - m}{0.0025}$

The mean must be 1.005 kg.

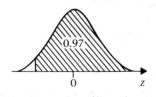

4 $\Phi(z) = 0.005$ $z = -2.575$
$$\frac{1.5 - 1.53}{\sigma} = -2.575$$
The standard deviation must be 0.0117.

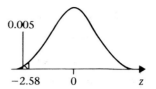

5 $\Phi(z) = 0.7$ $z = 0.524$
$$\frac{78 - 68}{\sigma} = 0.524$$
The standard deviation is 19.08.

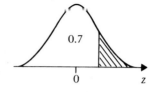

6 $z = \dfrac{140 - 125}{8} = 1.875$

$\Phi(1.875) = 0.970$ (to 3 s.f.).

3% of adult males have dangerously high blood pressure.

7 $\Phi(z) = 0.75$ $z = 0.675$
$$\frac{31 - 28}{\sigma} = 0.675$$
The standard deviation must be 4.44.

8 $\dfrac{498.5 - 500}{4} < z < \dfrac{500.5 - 500}{4}$

$-0.375 < z < 0.125$

19.6% of tubs will weigh between 498.5 g and 500.5 g.

9 $\dfrac{150 - 154.2}{5.1} < z < \dfrac{155 - 154.2}{5.1}$

$-0.824 < z < 0.157$

35.7% of the girls are between 150 cm and 155 cm tall.

10 $\Phi(z) = 0.9$ $z = 1.28$
$$\frac{70 - \mu}{\sigma} = 1.28$$

$\Phi(z) = 0.2$ $z = -0.84$
$$\frac{35 - \mu}{\sigma} = -0.84$$

The mean is 48.87 and the standard deviation is 16.51.

3 From binomial to Normal

3.1 Binomial to Normal

> What distribution does this remind you of?

It looks similar to the bell shape of the Normal distribution. This similarity will be explained in this chapter.

> What is the difference between a **discrete** and a **continuous** random variable?

A discrete random variable can take only certain distinct values, such as the number of children in a family or the number of cars passing a particular junction. A continuous random variable can take any value within a given range, for example the heights of all sixth-form pupils, or the length of time shoppers have to wait at the supermarket check-out.

3.2 Using the Normal to approximate binomial distributions

> Make a similar approximate calculation to show that when 1000 coins are thrown it is likely that between 470 and 530 heads will be obtained.

The number of heads $X \sim B(1000, 0.5)$

A Normal distribution with mean $= np = 500$ and variance $= npq = 250$ would model this distribution.

530 is **about** 2 standard deviations
above the mean:
$\Phi(2) = 0.977$ (from tables)

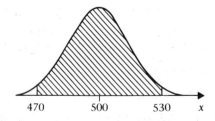

So there is a probability of approximately 95% that there will be between 470 and 530 heads. About 95% of the throws of 1000 coins would result in between 470 and 530 heads. You would be very unlikely to obtain a number of heads outside this range.

3.3 More detailed considerations

> What Normal distribution would you use to approximate $B(48, \frac{1}{4})$?

The Normal distribution would have $\quad$ mean $= np \ = 12$
$$\text{variance} = npq = \ 9$$
So $B(48, \frac{1}{4})$ is approximately $N(12, 9)$.

> Why is the area to the **right** of $z = 2.5$
> $\quad 1 - 0.994 = 0.006$?

Since the total area must be 1, the area to the right must be 1 minus the area to the left.

> Explain why a binomial distribution is an appropriate model for X.

Assume:

- that births are independent;

- there are only two possibilities (male or female);

- there is a fixed number of 'trials' $(n = 50)$.

Under such conditions a binomial model is appropriate.

Since $p = \frac{1}{2}$ and n is large (50), a Normal model will be a close fit to the binomial and you may use it to obtain the probabilities in this case.

EXERCISE 1

1 (a) $B(100, \frac{1}{2})$ is approximated by $N(50, 25)$
   $P(X \geqslant 52)$ is the area to the right of 51.5.
   $$z = \frac{51.5 - 50}{5} = 0.3$$
   $P(Z > 0.3) \ = 0.382$

   (b) $B(1000, \frac{1}{2})$ is approximated by $N(500, 250)$
   $P(X \geqslant 520)$ is the area to the right of 519.5.
   $$z = \frac{519.5 - 500}{\sqrt{250}} = 1.233$$
   $P(Z > 1.233) \ = 0.109$

   (c) $B(10\,000, \frac{1}{2})$ is approximated by $N(5000, 2500)$
   $P(X \geqslant 5200)$ is the area to the right of 5199.5.
   $$z = \frac{5199.5 - 5000}{50} = 3.99$$
   $P(Z > 3.99) = 0.000$

2 B(200, 0.7) is approximated by N(140, 42).
$$z = \frac{149.5 - 140}{\sqrt{42}} = 1.466$$
$$P(Z > 1.466) = 0.071$$

3 B(30, $\frac{1}{6}$) is approximated by N(5, 4.167).
P(X = 5) is the area between 4.5 and 5.5.
$$z = \frac{5.5 - 5}{\sqrt{4.167}} = 0.245$$
$$z = \frac{4.5 - 5}{\sqrt{4.167}} = -0.245$$
$$P(-0.245 < Z < 0.245) = 0.194$$

4 B(1000, 0.02) is approximated by N(20, 19.6).
$$z = \frac{20.5 - 20}{\sqrt{19.6}} = 0.1129$$
$$P(Z > 0.1129) = 0.455$$

5 B(1000, 0.15) is approximated by N(150, 127.5).

(a) P(X < 130) is the area to the left of 129.5.
$$z = \frac{129.5 - 150}{\sqrt{127.5}} = -1.816$$
$$P(Z < -1.816) = 0.035$$

(b) P(140 < X < 155) is the area between 140.5 and 154.5.
$$z = \frac{140.5 - 150}{\sqrt{127.5}} = -0.841$$
$$z = \frac{154.5 - 150}{\sqrt{127.5}} = 0.399$$
$$P(-0.841 < X < 0.399) = 0.455$$

6 B(75, 0.8) is approximated by N(60, 12).
P(X > 65) is the area to the right of 65.5.
$$z = \frac{65.5 - 60}{\sqrt{12}} = 1.588$$
$$P(Z > 1.588) = 0.0561$$

7 B(250, 0.24) is approximated by N(60, 45.6).
P(X < 55) is the area to the left of 54.5.
$$z = \frac{54.5 - 60}{\sqrt{45.6}} = -0.814$$
$$P(Z < -0.814) = 0.208$$

8 B(160, $\frac{3}{5}$) is approximated by N(96, 38.4).
P(90 < X < 100) is the area between 90.5 and 99.5.
$$z = \frac{90.5 - 96}{\sqrt{38.4}} = -0.888$$
$$z = \frac{99.5 - 96}{\sqrt{38.4}} = 0.565$$
$$P(-0.888 < Z < 0.565) = 0.527$$

9 B(200, 0.11) is approximated by N(22, 19.58).

(a) P(X < 20) is the area to the left of 19.5.

$$z = \frac{19.5 - 22}{\sqrt{19.58}} = -0.565 \cdot$$

$$P(Z < -0.565) = 0.286$$

(b) P(20 < X < 30) is the area between 20.5 and 29.5.

$$z = \frac{20.5 - 22}{\sqrt{19.58}} = -0.339$$

$$z = \frac{29.5 - 22}{\sqrt{19.58}} = 1.695$$

$$P(-0.339 < Z < 1.695) = 0.588$$

10 Boys: B(250, 0.186) is approximated by N(46.5, 37.851).
P(X > 50) is the area to the right of 50.5.

$$z = \frac{50.5 - 46.5}{\sqrt{37.851}} = 0.650$$

$$P(Z > 0.650) = 0.258$$

Girls: B(300, 0.189) is approximated by N(56.7, 45.98).
P(50 < X < 60) is the area between 50.5 and 59.5.

$$z = \frac{50.5 - 56.7}{\sqrt{45.98}} = -0.914 \qquad z = \frac{59.5 - 56.7}{\sqrt{45.98}} = 0.413$$

$$P(-0.914 < Z < 0.413) = 0.480$$

4 Sampling distribution of the mean

4.3 From population to sample

Check this using Normal tables.

The total of the unshaded areas $= 1 - 0.999 = 0.001$.
The area above $b = 0.0005$
and area below $b = 0.9995$.
From tables $\Phi(z) = 0.9995$
$\qquad z = 3.29$.

4.4 Sampling from other distributions

Explain why this value of z is taken.

The area under the Normal curve and below z is $97\frac{1}{2}\%$
i.e. $\Phi(z) = 0.975$
$\qquad z = 1.96$

EXERCISE 1

1 $X \sim N(166, 6^2)$ Sample size 5, $\bar{X} \sim N\left(166, \dfrac{6^2}{5}\right)$

$z = 1.49$
$P(-1.49 < Z < 1.49) = 0.864$

Sample size 8, $\bar{X} \sim N\left(166, \dfrac{6^2}{8}\right)$

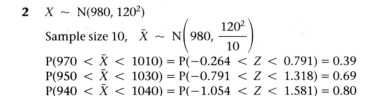

$z = 1.886$
$P(-1.886 < Z < 1.886) = 0.941$

162 166 170   cm

2 $X \sim N(980, 120^2)$

Sample size 10, $\bar{X} \sim N\left(980, \dfrac{120^2}{10}\right)$

$P(970 < \bar{X} < 1010) = P(-0.264 < Z < 0.791) = 0.39$
$P(950 < \bar{X} < 1030) = P(-0.791 < Z < 1.318) = 0.69$
$P(940 < \bar{X} < 1040) = P(-1.054 < Z < 1.581) = 0.80$

3 $X \sim N(162, 3.5^2)$

Sample size n, $\bar{X} \sim N\left(162, \dfrac{3.5^2}{n}\right)$

(a) $\dfrac{163.5 - 162}{3.5/\sqrt{n}} = 1.96$

$n = 20.9$
A sample of size 21 must be taken.

(b) $\dfrac{163 - 162}{3.5/\sqrt{n}} = 1.96$

$n = 47.06$
A sample of 48 must be taken.

4 $X \sim N(7.3, 0.078^2)$

Sample size n, $\bar{X} \sim N\left(7.3, \dfrac{0.078^2}{n}\right)$

(a) $\dfrac{7.33 - 7.3}{0.078/\sqrt{n}} = 1.96$

$n = 25.969$
A sample of 26 must be taken.

(b) $\dfrac{7.31 - 7.3}{0.078/\sqrt{n}} = 1.96$

$n = 233.72$
A sample of 234 must be taken.

5   N(250, 5^2) gives $\bar{X} \sim N\left(250, \dfrac{5^2}{10}\right)$

$$z = \frac{253 - 250}{5/\sqrt{10}} = 1.897$$

$$P(Z > 1.897) = 0.0289$$

6   (a) N(5.6, 0.4^2)

$$z = \frac{5.7 - 5.6}{0.4} = 0.25$$

$$P(Z > 0.25) = 0.401$$

(b) $\bar{X} \sim N\left(5.6, \dfrac{0.4^2}{12}\right)$

$$z = \frac{5.7 - 5.6}{0.04/\sqrt{12}} = 0.866$$

$$P(Z > 0.866) = 0.193$$

5 Estimating with confidence

5.1   How clean is our water?

> In which of the two cases would you be more confident of predicting the actual pH value of the water? Why?

The 12 samples which give mean values tightly bunched between 7.5 and 8.5 are more likely to indicate the actual pH level of the water. There is less variation in these results, which suggests that they are probably more accurate.

The other set of results has mean values more widely spread and you should feel less confident about using these to predict the actual pH value.

5.2   The standard error

> Calculate the standard errors of the other two sample means for Clean Valley water. Write them in $\bar{x}$ (n, s.e.) form, as above.

Clean Valley Primary School:

$$n = 25, \quad \text{variance of } \bar{x} = \frac{0.5}{n} = 0.02$$

$\bar{x} = 8.5 \quad (n = 25, \text{ s.e.} = \sqrt{0.02} = 0.141)$

Clean Valley Water Authority

$$n = 100, \quad \text{variance of } \bar{x} = \frac{0.5}{n} = 0.005$$

$\bar{x} = 8.3 \quad (n = 100, \text{ s.e.} = \sqrt{0.005} = 0.071)$

EXERCISE 1

1 (a) 0.4   (b) 0.095

2 (a) $\bar{x} = 5.57$ $n = 6$ s.e. = 0.816

   (b) $\bar{x} = 6.75$ $n = 20$ s.e. = 0.447

3 $\bar{x} = 3.7$ $n = 40$ s.e. = 0.079

   3 s.e. above the mean would give a value of 3.94.
   This is still well below the normal pH of 5.7, which suggests that there is
   excess acid in the rain.

5.3 Confidence intervals

> What evidence do you have for this figure?

The distribution of sample means is Normal. You know from earlier work
that approximately 68% of all possible values lie within 1 standard
deviation of the mean value.

> If you increase your degree of confidence, what happens to the
> confidence interval?

Not unexpectedly, the confidence interval gets wider. You can say with
certainty, for example, that the height of adult females in England is
between 0 and 500 cm!

> Calculate a 68% interval and comment on the widths of the 95% and
> 68% intervals.

The 68% interval is (8.04, 8.36). It is much smaller than the 95% interval.

EXERCISE 2

1 (a) Clean Valley Primary School:

$$\bar{x} = 8.15 \quad n = 25 \quad \sigma^2 = 0.5$$

$$\text{s.e.} = \frac{\sigma}{\sqrt{n}} = 0.141$$

68% confidence interval (8.01, 8.29)
95% confidence interval (7.87, 8.43)

(b) Clean Valley Water Authority:

$$\bar{x} = 7.8 \quad n = 100 \quad \sigma^2 = 0.5$$

$$\text{s.e.} = \frac{\sigma}{\sqrt{n}} = 0.071$$

68% confidence interval (7.73, 7.87)
95% confidence interval (7.66, 7.94)

2

	68%	95%
(a)	(4.75, 6.39)	(3.94, 7.20)
(b)	(6.30, 7.20)	(5.86, 7.64)

3 $(\bar{x} - 3 \text{ s.e.}, \bar{x} + 3 \text{ s.e.})$ gives a 99.7% confidence interval.

5.4 Other intervals

Use Normal tables to find z, where $\Phi(z) = 0.95$.

$$\Phi(z) = 0.95 \Rightarrow z = 1.645$$

Show that the **95% confidence interval** for μ is
$(\bar{x} - 1.96 \text{ s.e.}, \bar{x} + 1.96 \text{ s.e.})$.

Calculate the corresponding 99% confidence interval.

$\Phi(z) = 0.975$
$\Rightarrow z = 1.96.$

Similarly for 99% confidence interval $\Phi(z) = 0.995$
$$\Rightarrow z = 2.58$$
$(\bar{x} - 2.58 \text{ s.e.}, \bar{x} + 2.58 \text{ s.e.})$ is the 99% confidence interval.

EXERCISE 3

1 $n = 9$ $\sigma = 10$ $\bar{x} = 20$ s.e. = 3.33

90% confidence interval (14.52, 25.48)
95% confidence interval (13.47, 26.53)
99% confidence interval (11.41, 28.59)

2 The confidence intervals would be smaller.
$n = 25$ $\sigma = 10$ $\bar{x} = 20$ s.e. = 2

90% confidence interval (16.71, 23.29)
95% confidence interval (16.08, 23.92)
99% confidence interval (14.84, 25.16)

3 (a) (12.59, 13.61)

(b) (2.53, 2.77)

(c) (201.62, 208.38)

4 (a) (0.0999, 0.160)

(b) (20.51, 21.29)

(c) (842.3, 847.7)

5 Sample: $n = 50$ $\bar{x} = 26$ $\sigma^2 = 6$

$$\text{s.e.} = \frac{\sqrt{6}}{\sqrt{50}} = 0.346$$

The 95% confidence interval is 26 ± 1.96 s.e.
i.e. (25.3, 26.7)

6 $\sigma = 9.5$ $n = 10$ s.e. = 3.004 $\bar{x} = 117.1$

90% confidence interval (112.16, 122.04)

7 (a) Width of 95% confidence interval is 3.92;

(b) width of 95% confidence interval is 2.77;

(c) width of 95% confidence interval is 1.96.

For a width of 1, a sample of 1537 would have to be taken.

5.5 Estimating a population variance

> Check that $\sigma^2 = 1$.

This can be checked simply by using the statistics functions on your calculator. Alternatively:

x	-1	1
$x - \mu$	-1	1
$(x - \mu)^2$	1	1
$P(X = x)$	$\frac{1}{2}$	$\frac{1}{2}$

$$\sigma^2 = 1 \times \frac{1}{2} + 1 \times \frac{1}{2} = 1$$

> When $n = 3$, show that the mean of the distribution of sample variances is $\frac{2}{3}$.

$$\frac{1}{4} \times 0 + \frac{3}{4} \times \frac{8}{9} = \frac{2}{3}$$

EXERCISE 4

1 (a) $s^2 = 0.0016$, $\left(\dfrac{n}{n-1}\right) s^2 = 0.0019$ (b) $s^2 = 33.05$, $\left(\dfrac{n}{n-1}\right) s^2 = 36.72$

2 (a) $s^2 = 2.038$, $\left(\dfrac{n}{n-1}\right) s^2 = 2.061$ (b) $s^2 = 1829$, $\left(\dfrac{n}{n-1}\right) s^2 = 1925$

3 Estimate of mean is 1.501
Sample variance $\approx 8.2 \times 10^{-6}$
Estimate of σ^2 is 9.9×10^{-6}

5.6 Populations with unknown variance

> Are these reasonable assumptions? What can you do if they are not?

You know from the previous chapter that the distribution of the sample mean is Normal whatever the parent population, provided the sample size is large enough.

In the examples you have considered so far, the variance of the population was known. In practice you would not always know the variance of the population and it may be necessary to find an estimate for it.

> For the remission data above, calculate 95% confidence limits for the
> population mean, using (i) s_n^2, (ii) s_{n-1}^2 as an estimator for the
> population variance.

$n = 29 \quad \bar{x} = 13.59 \quad s_n^2 = 8.826^2 \quad s_{n-1}^2 = 8.982^2$

(i) 95% confidence interval $\left(13.59 - 1.96\left(\dfrac{8.826}{\sqrt{29}}\right), 13.59 + 1.96\left(\dfrac{8.826}{\sqrt{29}}\right)\right)$

$= (10.38, 16.80)$

(ii) 95% confidence interval $\left(13.59 - 1.96\left(\dfrac{8.982}{\sqrt{29}}\right), 13.59 + 1.96\left(\dfrac{8.982}{\sqrt{29}}\right)\right)$

$= (10.32, 16.86)$

EXERCISE 5

1 (a) Population variance (estimated) $= \dfrac{n}{n-1} s_n^2 = \dfrac{36}{35} \times 4 = 4.11$

A 95% interval is 10 ± 1.96 s.e. $= 10 \pm 1.96 \dfrac{\sigma}{\sqrt{n}}$

$= 10 \pm 1.96 \times 0.338$

$= (9.34, 10.7)$ to 3 s.f.

(b) Population variance (estimated) $= \dfrac{100}{99} \times 9 = 9.09$

A 95% interval is 20 ± 1.96 s.e. $= 20 \pm 1.96 \times 0.301$

$= (19.4, 20.6)$, to 3 s.f.

(c) Population variance (estimated) $= \dfrac{5}{4} \times (0.01) = 0.0125$

A 95% interval is 20 ± 1.96 s.e. $= 20 \pm 1.96 \times 0.05$

$= (19.9, 20.1)$ to 3 s.f.

The answer is likely to be inaccurate because the sample size is small.

2 $n = 59 \quad \bar{x} = 114 \quad s_{n-1} = 4.14 \quad$ s.e. $= 0.538$
A 90% confidence interval is $(113, 115)$ to 3 s.f.

3 $n = 891 \quad \bar{x} = 3.856 \quad s_{n-1} = 1.286 \quad$ s.e. $= 0.043$
A 95% confidence interval is $(3.77, 3.94)$

The actual mean age of the fish is unknown. However, this single sample
provides an interval which you can be confident contains the mean, since if
you took a large number of samples of this size, **each** would generate **its own**
confidence interval for the mean. 95% of these would contain the true mean.

4 (a) $n = 10 \quad \bar{x} = 10 \quad s_{n-1} = 4.22 \quad$ s.e. $= 1.33$
A 90% confidence interval is $(7.8, 12.2)$

(b) The sample is small, so you can only say that the distribution of sample
means is approximately Normal.

6 Population proportions

6.1 How many are there?

> Explain why the estimated number of fish in the lake is $\dfrac{50n}{x}$.

You must assume that the proportion of marked fish in the catch is the same as in the lake as a whole.

$$\frac{x}{50} = \frac{n}{N} \Rightarrow N = \frac{50n}{x}$$

6.2 Opinion polls

> Explain why X has this distribution.

A member of the population chosen at random has probability p of voting Conservative. Since the population is very large, this probability is (virtually) the same for each member of the sample independently of the voting intentions of other members of the sample.

The distribution of X is therefore that of a binomial with 400 trials and probability of success p.

> Carefully show how inequality ② can be deduced from inequality ①.

Part of inequality ① is:

$$400p - 1.96 \sqrt{400p\,(1-p)} < X$$

$$\Rightarrow \qquad 400p < X + 1.96 \sqrt{400p\,(1-p)}$$

$$\Rightarrow \qquad p < \frac{X}{400} + 1.96 \sqrt{\frac{p(1-p)}{400}}$$

The other half of inequality ① is:

$$X < 400p + 1.96 \sqrt{400p\,(1-p)}$$

$$\Rightarrow X - 1.96 \sqrt{400p\,(1-p)} < 400p$$

$$\Rightarrow \frac{X}{400} - 1.96 \sqrt{\frac{p(1-p)}{400}} < p$$

Combining the two inequalities for p gives inequality ②.

EXERCISE 1

1 (a) (i) For males, the 95% confidence interval is $0.67 \pm 1.96 \sqrt{\dfrac{0.67 \times 0.33}{444}}$

i.e. 0.63 to 0.71

(ii) For females, the interval is $0.72 \pm 1.96 \sqrt{\dfrac{0.72 \times 0.28}{360}}$ i.e. 0.67 to 0.77

(b) $0.19 \pm 1.645 \sqrt{\dfrac{0.19 \times 0.81}{313}}$ = 0.154 to 0.226

2 (a) 12 out of 30 are marked. The point estimate of the proportion marked is $\dfrac{12}{30} = 0.4$

Confidence interval: $0.4 \pm 1.96 \sqrt{\dfrac{0.4 \times 0.6}{30}}$ i.e. 0.22 to 0.58

(b) The estimated number of fish in the lake is N.

The upper limit for N is $\dfrac{50}{0.22} = 227$

and the lower limit for N is $\dfrac{50}{0.58} = 86$

There are between 86 and 227 fish in the lake.

3 (a) Point estimate $p = 0.5$
The council requires $p \pm 0.02$
The 90% interval for p is $p \pm 1.645$ s.e.

$1.645 \sqrt{\dfrac{0.5 \times 0.5}{n}} \le 0.02$

$\Rightarrow n \ge 1691$
The council should select a sample of at least 1691 people.

(b) $0.02 \ge 1.96 \sqrt{\dfrac{0.5 \times 0.5}{n}}$

$\Rightarrow n \ge 2401$

MATHEMATICS DEPARTMENT

BARTON PEVERIL COLLEGE

CEDAR ROAD

EASTLEIGH